BLOODY BR

HISTOR

YORK

A city built on bones: Roman coffins recycled as garden ornaments in the Museum Gardens.

BLOODY BRITISH HISTORY

HISTORY

YORK

CHRISTINA SURDHAR

First published in 2013

The History Press
The Mill, Brimscombe Port
Stroud, Gloucestershire, GL5 2QG
www.thehistorypress.co.uk

British Library Cataloguing in Publication Data.
A catalogue record for this book is available from the British Library.

ISBN 978 0 7524 9105 9

Typesetting and origination by The History Press
Printed and bound by TJ International Ltd, Padstow, Cornwall

CONTENTS

ORIGINS OF YORK

THE MILITARY FORTRESS OF EBORACUM

Even in the beginning there was fighting and bloodshed. York was not founded as a town, but as a Roman military fortress, from which the 5,000 crack troops of the IX Legion Hispana could crush the local tribes, the Brigantes, and take their territory for Rome.

It was decided to build the fortress on undeveloped land at the meeting point of two rivers, the Foss and the Ouse, and it was a perfect location for the purpose. It had excellent communications via land as well as river for the transport of men and supplies and there were farms nearby which would be able to supply food. It was close to the border of the Brigantes' territory and that of their

The Multangular Tower, one of the two huge corner towers attached to the front of the military fortress after it was rebuilt in stone. The original Roman brickwork can still be seen on the lower part.

Romans in battle with barbarians.

neighbouring tribe, the Parisii, which perhaps made it more neutral. And importantly, it was also ideally situated for launching strikes on rebel outposts in the Pennines and the North York Moors.

So in AD 71, the fortress known as Eboracum (Celtic meaning: 'place of the yew trees') was built by the river Ouse. Within its walls were barracks, an administrative headquarters, a forum, a bath house and workshops. The fortress established the location of York's future town centre and some of the streets of today's city. Once the fortress was built, the superior weaponry and military tactics of the Roman army could be brought to bear on the Brigantes.

The Brigantes had not always been the Romans' enemies. Their queen Cartimandua was a Roman ally, but her husband Venutius, a powerful warlord in his own right, did not share her Roman sympathies. Gradually, with encouragement from Venutius, Cartimandua's people turned against her. Trouble first broke out in AD 51 when she turned the British rebel leader Caractacus over to Rome. Then, in AD 69, a new scandal involving the queen led to her downfall. Cartimandua was having a very public affair with the armour bearer of her husband. With the support of the people, whose sympathy lay on his side, Venutius launched an attack on Cartimandua. The Romans managed to rescue her, but only just, leaving a now hostile people on the borders of their conquered territory. It was a situation which could not be allowed to persist.

Enter the IX Legion, under the command of Petilius Cerialis. Although there are no detailed accounts of those first bloody campaigns against the Brigantes, we do have the following summary:

> Petilius Cerialis struck terror by an attack upon the Brigantes, who are reputed to compose the most populous state in the whole province. Many battles were fought, some of them attended with much bloodshed; and the greater part of the Brigantes were either brought into subjection or involved in the ravages of war.
>
> (Tacitus, *Agricola*, 17)

The Brigantes were certainly up against a formidable foe. The Roman army was highly professional, its infantry soldiers trained to fight together as a single unit, a veritable killing machine. Each soldier was armed with a dagger or pugio, a short sword or gladius, a semi-cylindrical shield, the scutum, and two javelins, or pila. Both pila would be thrown one after the other at the beginning of battle, and would bend on impact with the enemies' shields, rendering them useless so they would have to be discarded. Then the Romans would move in, marching forward, shoulder to shoulder in tight formation. They used their shields to knock their opponents off balance and then stabbed with the gladius, thrusting forward horizontally rather than stabbing, aiming for internal organs through rib cages. Once fallen, the Romans trampled the enemy under foot with hobnail sandals. After the initial rout by the foot soldiers, the cavalry moved in to complete the attack.

In this way the Brigantes were conquered. As each area fell and its people were brought to submission, Roman towns were established throughout the region, including an administrative centre for the Brigantes at Aldborough.

THE MYSTERY OF THE LOST LEGION

Not long after founding York, the IX Legion Hispana famously disappeared from history. In a document compiled in the AD 160s which lists all serving regiments, the IX is not mentioned. It has apparently vanished, or ceased to exist.

This disappearance is one which has captured people's imagination ever since it was made famous by Rosemary Sutcliffe's 1954 novel *The Eagle of the Ninth*. According to the novel, the legion was sent north on campaign to Scotland, where it was brutally wiped out by native tribes. In the 1950s this was thought to be a reasonable historical explanation. More recently, historians have argued that the IX was strategically transferred to Holland, and later Palestine, where it met with its bloody end. But now, some academics are questioning the evidence for the new theory, and believe it is more likely the legion was annihilated in Britain after all.

The last place to which the IX Legion can be accurately dated is York in AD 108; its name is mentioned on an inscription commemorating the completion of building work. But by AD 122 we know it had left the city, as the XI Legion Victrix arrived at Eboracum as the new garrisoning force. What ultimately became of the IX Legion is still the biggest mystery of Roman Britain. But it was 'last seen' in York, the city it founded.

Roman stamp: one of several objects in the Yorkshire Museum relating to the IX Legion.
(© York Museums Trust, Yorkshire Museum)

DAILY LIFE IN ROMAN YORK

GRISLY GLADIATORS AND BLOODY RELIGION

As the Roman military fortress became established at Eboracum, a thriving civilian town grew up on the opposite bank of the river Ouse. By the early third century, it was given the high Roman town status of *colonia* and was the capital of Britannia Inferior, the northern part of the province (the word inferior refers to the greater distance of the north from Rome, while the south, being closer, was Britannia Superior).

The colonia of Eboracum was an impressive and sophisticated place, with residential houses in both wood and stone, temples, a baths complex, a good drainage system, food storage facilities, and busy workshops. But it was also a place which would be in many ways quite alien to us today, a place where violence and a certain amount of blood and gore went with the territory and the time.

Nowhere is this more evident than in one of the Romans' favourite spectator events: the gladiatorial combat. Gladiators were fearsomely armed, highly trained slaves, who battled to the death in the arena for the entertainment of the public. Although an amphitheatre has never been found in York, it is almost certain that there will have been one in such a large and important town. But a recent discovery has provided other evidence for

---

BURIED BABY IN BLAKE STREET

In Blake Street, under the remains of a Roman military barrack block, archaeologists found the body of a human infant, most likely buried as a votive offering to the gods during the construction of the building. It is assumed, but not known for sure, that the baby had already died of natural causes. It was common for Romans to bury the bodies of babies inside houses, as they were not yet considered to be fully human, and therefore did not need to be buried in a cemetery. But it is unusual to find one in a military fortress, which is why this is thought to be a votive burial.

Roman arena. The location of the Roman arena in York is unknown, but it is thought that it could be under the Yorkshire Museum.

gladiators in York, in the form of some rather grisly human remains.

In 2004-2005, excavations in Driffield Terrace on the south-western outskirts of the town unearthed eighty skeletons from the Roman period, almost all of them male. They were taller and more heavily built than most men of the time, and their bones showed signs of gruesome injuries. Forty-five had been decapitated and twenty had suffered other kinds of violent death. At first it was thought that the men could have been executed soldiers – but then other, more unusual, features started to suggest a different explanation. These men, it seemed, were very possibly gladiators, brutally killed in the arena for the entertainment of the citizens of Roman York.

Some of the men had been killed with a hammer blow to the head, a way that wounded or dying gladiators were often dispatched, by a slave dressed as the god of the underworld. And one, very

significantly, had been bitten around the hip by a large animal such as a lion, tiger or bear. Man *vs* animal fights were common in the arena, performed by specialised gladiators called *bestiariii* or *venatores*. Around a third of the bodies had one arm significantly longer than the other, suggesting one-sided work such as sword practice from an early age. It is interesting, also, that all the bodies had been buried carefully, along with grave goods such as food and pottery vessels, unlike normal victims of execution. This could fit with the gladiator theory as gladiators were revered by society, despite their slave status and bloody exploits. Whether these men were actually gladiators is not known for sure, but much of the evidence certainly seems to point to it.

Bloodiness in Roman York was not just confined to the amphitheatre, however. It also played a part in religion, which was an important part of daily life. The soldiers at the military fortress will

SEVERE SEVERUS

In AD 208 the Roman Emperor Septimius Severus took up residence in York with his family, elite guard and extensive entourage. Severus was a ruthless ruler. When faced with a rebellion during his time in York he ordered his army to march north, killing every Briton they encountered: 'Let no one escape total destruction at our hands, not even the child carried in its mother's womb.'

Severus's purpose in York was to conquer the territories north of Hadrian's Wall for Rome – something he could not achieve, despite numerous campaigns. When he became ill and was forced to retire from military campaigning, Severus urged his son Caracalla to battle on. But Caracalla, aware that his father was going to die, was more interested in seizing the imperial crown. Septimius Severus died in York on 4 February AD 211. According to one source, his death was 'not without a certain amount of help, it is said, from Caracalla.'

have attended compulsory ceremonies, where the commander, as the Emperor's representative, presided over ritual animal sacrifices. Once an animal was killed, the fortress's *haruspex*, a priest who practised divination, will have examined its entrails to see what they foretold. Less gorily, the fortress's augur foretold the future by studying the flight of birds. But when the soldiers were off duty, they could take part in whatever religious practices they chose, and there were many temples in Eboracum.

The town was a centre for several of the mystery cults which became popular in the second and third centuries, one of which was that of the fertility goddess Cybele. According to the myth of Cybele, her lover was the shepherd boy Atys. He was unfaithful and castrated himself to express his remorse. The priests of the cult of Cybele would also ritually castrate themselves as an act of devotion. A fragment of a monument depicting Atys was found in The Mount in York. The mystery cults of

Roman Mithraic relief from Micklegate, one of the many interesting objects from York's Roman past on display in the Yorkshire Museum. The slaughter of a bull is central to the mystery cult of Mithras. (© York Museums Trust, Yorkshire Museum)

Isis and Mithras were also practised in the town and a temple to Isis's consort Serapis was located near the baths in the civilian *colonia*.

VIKINGS TAKE YORK

KING AELLE MOST HORRIBLY MURDERED

On 1 November 866, the Vikings took York. The 'Great Heathen Army', thought to have numbered as many as 10-15,000 men, was led by Ivar the Boneless and his brother Halfdan. And this attack was different from the many Viking raids which had occurred over the past century. The invading army was not just after booty: its aim was to seize power and to stay here, as the rulers of England.

Ivar the Boneless was a fearsome warlord, described by his contemporaries as 'most cruel' and 'never having lost a battle'. His strange nickname, 'the boneless', is not fully understood, but historians have considered a variety of possible explanations for it, from brittle bone disease to impotence. Whatever the case, Ivar was certainly not an impotent force when it came to warfare.

The reason for the conquest of England, according to the Viking sagas, was to avenge the death of Ivar and Halfdan's father Ragnar, at the hands of King Aelle of Northumbria. York – or Eorfwic, as it was called by the Anglo-Saxons – was at the heart of the kingdom of Northumbria, a territory

The Viking raiders strike in York.

which stretched upwards from the river Humber, through the north-east of England and to the Forth in Scotland. York was the seat of the Northumbrian kings, and also of archbishops who wielded a considerable amount of power. According to the scholar Alcuin, York was also an 'emporium' full of the fruits of trade, both at home and with lands overseas. Vengeance aside, it was a tempting prize for the Vikings.

Ivar and his army attacked York on All Saints' Day, a day when leaders and dignitaries would be there to attend church, and could be all dealt with together. According to the *Anglo-Saxon Chronicle*, 'they sought the enemy at York, and broke into the town, and some of them got in and there was an unmeasurable slaughter of Northumbrians; some inside, some outside; and both kings were slain.'

The Viking sagas recount how Ivar and Halfdan had their revenge on King Aelle. He was the victim of the 'blood eagle', a gruesome, stomach-churning ritual sacrifice to the god Odin, where a living person had his back opened up, his ribcage cut open, and his lungs pulled out of his back to look like bloody eagle's wings, still inflated and moving; 'all his ribs were severed from the backbone with a sword, so that his lungs were pulled out'. As Sighvat says in the poem *Knutsdrapa*:

Ivar he who
held court at York,
had eagle hacked
in Ella's back.

York was taken, brutally and swiftly. But the conquest did not stop there. The Great Heathen Army continued its rampage in the south, and went on to force the kingdoms of Mercia (the Midlands) and East Anglia into submission. In 876, part of the army returned to York. The Vikings rebuilt the town and settled in it, and Halfdan shared out the lands of the Northumbrians. In 878 a truce was agreed with Alfred, the Saxon King of Wessex, by which the Vikings now officially governed an immense territory. It was known as the Danelaw. York, renamed Jorvik, was its most important city – the capital of the Vikings in England.

Jorvik grew and continued to prosper under its new rulers. But how did the vicious Vikings suddenly settle down? Did they somehow become 'civilised' overnight? The archaeological discoveries made on the site of the new shopping centre at Coppergate in the late 1970s transformed the way we think about the Vikings, not just in York, but throughout the country. The bloodthirsty warrior of the Icelandic sagas had previously been the predominant image, but suddenly evidence was discovered for a much more peaceful way of life. The dig unearthed Viking homes, games, jewellery, and signs of thriving cottage industries. A reconstruction of a Coppergate street scene, complete with people going about their daily lives, can be seen today in York at the Jorvik Viking Centre.

It can be difficult to fit these very different images of Vikings together. But not everyone in Viking society was a warrior, and when warriors were not out raping, pillaging and looting monasteries, hard as it might be to imagine, they also had homes

Viking warrior, as depicted in the Lewis Chess Set.

weapons in steel of a quality not seen again until the Industrial Revolution. It is significant that the great symbol of power, Thor's hammer, was a blacksmith's hammer used in the forging of weaponry. And Viking kings were always expected to be great war leaders. Even as Vikings became Christians, they did not forget their heritage, as is shown by the image of an armed warrior on a stone cross at St Andrew's church in Middleton, near York.

While some Vikings might have seemed to be settling down, others continued raiding in the South into the 900s. And the power struggle at the top was continuous throughout the period. Kings were constantly being overthrown and replaced by other kings. Jorvik's ordinary people must have learnt to cope with these very unstable times. In fact, not only were they able to live with political upheavals, violence and revolution: they managed to thrive.

and families. But there is no doubt that traditional Viking culture was linked closely with conquest and warfare. Viking blacksmiths, who were regarded with an almost religious respect, made

ERIC BLOODAXE

THE LAST KING OF YORK

Eric Bloodaxe, son of King Harold Finehair, was every bit as ferocious as the name suggests. Kicked out of Norway for murdering both his brothers in a dispute over the throne, Eric set sail into what could have been a lonely exile – but instead became an extended plundering trip around northern Europe. Then, in AD 947, he received an interesting invitation.

York's Anglo-Scandinavian 'witan' invited Eric Bloodaxe to become the King of Northumbria. This move on their part was not as wise as a decision as you might expect for what was essentially a council of wise men. It was not his bloodthirsty nature which could be a problem – they clearly saw this as an advantage, hoping Eric would bring York back to its glory days of ruthless Viking rulers. The problem was that they already had a king. Just months before, albeit reluctantly, they had formally submitted to the sovereignty of King Eadred, the Anglo-Saxon King of England, bringing him tribute and gifts to mark his acceptance. This was conveniently forgotten when they learned Eric was on the move, and looking for a new kingdom.

Eric accepted the witan's invitation and arrived in York to be crowned king. York's royal moneyers, who had previously minted Eadred's currency, were now minting coins boldly declaring the kingship of another: Eric Rex.

Eric's royal hall was right in the centre of town, surrounded on all sides by typical wooden dwellings of the time. It was not far from today's King's Square, whose name still references it. The hall is mentioned in the sagas as the 'King's Garth' and King's Square was still known as *Kuningsgard* in the thirteenth century. The huge south-eastern gatehouse of the Roman fortress was also in this area, an impressive building with great arches, and it is possible Eric's

A witan, or Anglo-Saxon council of wise men, here shown with the king presiding. York's witan accepted Eadred as king, then abandoned him for Eric Bloodaxe.

hall could have been built into what was remaining of it in this period. Here, he would have sat at his table, surrounded by his royal court and his following of armed men.

King Eric Bloodaxe is described in *Egil's Saga*:

> Under a helmet of terror, the all-powerful lord of the people sat over the land and gave lavish gifts. The king ruled in York with harsh thought for his sea-washed shores.
>
> It was not safe, nor without terror, to look at the light of Eric's eye, when serpent keen, the eye of the all-powerful shone with terrifying light.

Unfortunately, it did not take long for trouble to erupt. King Eadred took his revenge in the summer of 948, riding to Northumbria, and setting about a campaign of terror. According to John of Wallingford, Eadred 'burned down towns, razed fortifications, slaughtered opposition and arrested suspects.' Eadred also destroyed St Wilfred's Minster at Ripon, an act which outraged the north and even shocked the south.

With large areas of Northumbria laid to waste, Eadred headed back southwards, but Eric Bloodaxe was not going to let him go without a fight – or rather, a slaughter. Eric led an army from York to the ford crossing of the Aire at Castleford. There he lay in wait at the narrow road which led to the ford, and when Eadred's rear guard came along he all but annihilated it. Eadred was enraged, and threatened to return to destroy Northumbria completely. Fearful of Eadred's wrath, the Northumbrians expelled Eric

Re-enactor at York Viking Festival. (© Andy Whale)

Bloodaxe and accepted the Anglo-Saxon king again.

Eric's first reign in York had lasted only one year, but by 952, the *Anglo-Saxon Chronicle* tells us Eric Bloodaxe was back again at the King's Garth in Jorvik. His second reign lasted almost three years, until his death in 954. Eric was finally killed in battle at 'a lonely place called Stainmore' along with his son Haeric and his brother Ragnald. His death marked the end of independent northern rule. According to John of Wallingford's chronicle, 'From that time to the present, Northumbria has been grieving for want of a king of its own, and for the liberty they once enjoyed.'

So what was it like to live in the capital of Northumbria at the time of Eric Bloodaxe? In the late 900s, Jorvik was at the centre of a trading network which stretched across the world. The Vikings imported amber from the Baltic, wine from northern Europe, silks from the Middle East, and furs from Scandinavia. Evidence for large scale trading of this kind has been recently unearthed in excavations at Hungate. Archaeologists have found an area of Jorvik which seems to have been reserved for traders, consisting of organised rows

ERIC BLOODAXE'S YORK

York at the time of Eric Bloodaxe was one of the most prosperous and exciting places to be. A contemporary writer describes it as '...indescribably rich, packed with the goods of merchants who come from all over but especially from the Danes, a multitude of people numbering 30,000, not counting infants.'

of warehouses and not far from the rivers where boats would arrive with their cargos. Workshops in the city also provided goods for export.

As well as riches and prosperity, however, there was also filth and squalor. The leather workers' quarter, which was near where Lloyds Bank stands in Pavement today, was a stinking area of workshops where skin was stripped from carcasses of animals, and chicken dung and urine were used in the manufacturing process. And in the wattle and daub houses where people lived, rubbish was disposed of in the back yards, where pigs and other animals were also kept. We know, from archaeologists' examination of human faeces from the period, that many inhabitants of Jorvik were infested with intestinal worms, caused by unhygienic living conditions.

Eric's York was a place of contradictions which are unfathomable to us today: political turbulence and thriving trade, opulence and squalor. And in the midst of it all, both in York and in the wider region of Northumbria, a specific culture was emerging. The people there, a mix of Anglo-Saxons, Danes, Norwegians and Celts, were becoming the very first 'Northerners'.

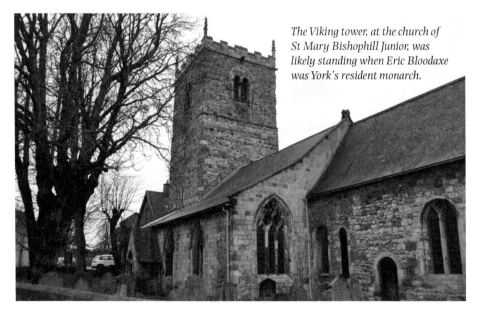

The Viking tower, at the church of St Mary Bishophill Junior, was likely standing when Eric Bloodaxe was York's resident monarch.

20 SEPTEMBER 1066

THE BATTLE OF FULFORD

A GIANT VIKING DESCENDS ON YORK

In September 1066 there was only one month until the Battle of Hastings would be fought in the south, but of course no-one knew this yet. In fact Harold Godwinson, King of England, had just disbanded his men; it looked to him like the threat of an invasion by William of Normandy had passed for the year. He was very wrong, as we now know, and in the north there was trouble of a different kind on the horizon.

The trouble took the form of a Viking, and a very large one at that if contemporary estimates of his size are to be believed. Harald Hardrada, King of Norway, stood five ells high according to one source. Five ells (or 7ft 6in) is perhaps an exaggeration, but it is nonetheless probable that he was exceptionally tall. And he was heading for York. Like Duke William of Normandy, Hardrada too had a claim to the English throne. He also had a very powerful ally: Tostig Godwinson, brother of King Harold of England, who was bitter at having had the earldom of Northumbria taken from him.

King Harald Hardrada, whose nickname means 'severe counsellor' or 'ruthless', was a Viking in the true sense of the word. A pirate and a raider, he lived to wage war, and had been doing so for most of his life. Exiled from his country at the age of fifteen, Hardrada had become a mercenary soldier, and grew rich from plundering and raiding in Russia and the Mediterranean. In 1047 he had returned to Norway, raised an army with his wealth, and reclaimed the throne after seven long years of fighting. In the years that followed, he had fought a bloody war against the Danes.

In 1066, Harald Hardrada's claim to the throne of England was somewhat vague – he had apparently been promised the Crown during the reign of King Harthacnut – but his invasion is likely to have been the result of opportunity as much as anything else. However, he had plenty of support from the Viking parts of the British Isles and a useful ally in Tostig Godwinson, who knew Northumbria well.

After a rendezvous at the mouth of the Tyne in the late summer of 1066, Harald Hardrada and Tostig Godwinson set sail for York, the seat of power in the north and the capital of Northumbria.

Fulford sign, commemorating the battle in the York suburb where it was fought.

Their vast fleet of warships must have been a terrifying sight to those who saw it approaching along the Yorkshire coastline. This was the largest scale Viking invasion ever to take place, with hundreds of ships, carrying thousands of men. On their way they stopped at Scarborough and Holderness, burning and destroying both settlements before setting out again along the Humber.

Northumbria was now ruled by Tostig's bitter rival, Earl Morcar of the house of Leofric. Morcar, together with his brother Edwin Earl of Mercia, had managed to summon some 5,000 men to defend York. This was no mean feat considering there will only have been a few days in which to do so. Harald Hardrada and Tostig moored their ships 10 miles from York at Riccall, and marched on the city, intending to capture it.

The Northern Earls, not wanting to risk a siege, moved their men out along the causeways from York to Fulford, 'the foul ford', so that on arrival there Hardrada found his way blocked. The two armies faced one another across a tributary of the river Ouse, now known as Germany Beck. More and more of Hardrada and Tostig's men arrived from Riccall as the hostile face-off continued. The Anglo-Saxons realised they were going to have to lead the offensive sooner, rather than later.

In a clash of shield walls, the two armies met. The battle was muddy and wet, fought on very marshy ground where the terrain made retreat and escape difficult, if not impossible. For a time the English had the upper hand, but after much arduous fighting Hardrada's men began to push them back. One flank of the English army, separated from

FALLEN SOLDIERS OF THE PAST

When the cemetery of St Andrew's church in Fishergate was excavated by the York Archaeological Trust, an interesting group of eleventh-century male burials was found. The skeletons were noticeable for having injuries consistent with those sustained in battle – sword cuts to arm and leg bones, point injuries caused by spear thrusts and arrows, and cracked or decapitated skulls. As St Andrew's was the nearest church to the site of battle at Fuford, it is possible that these are the remains of some of Edwin and Morcar's men, slain on 20 September 1066.

the other, managed to escape back to York. The other flank was not so lucky, completely surrounded and attempting to fight their way out. The result was a massacre. Many of those who were not hacked to death were crushed underfoot into the boggy ground. The Viking sagas say that the beck was running with blood. Perhaps the most haunting image from the sources of the time is the description of the slain men in the marsh making a pathway for the victorious Vikings, who were able to walk over them dry shod:

Earl Waltheof's men lay in the fen,
By sword down hewed, so thickly strewed,
That Norsemen say they paved a way
Across the fen for the brave Norsemen.

At the time, the Ouse was a tidal river, and as the tide began to rise the bodies would have begun to float. This may explain why there are references to many 'drowned' men at the battle site.

York now had no choice but to submit to Harald Hardrada, and on Sunday 24 September the city gates were opened to him. There, he held a 'Thing' (assembly) and the people of York were forced to pay him homage.

25 SEPTEMBER 1066

THE BATTLE OF STAMFORD BRIDGE

KING HAROLD TO THE RESCUE

Five days after their victory at the Battle of Fulford, the armies of Viking Harald Hardrada and his ally Tostig Godwinson were at Stamford Bridge, 7 miles east of York, waiting to receive hostages. It was a warm, summer-like day, and many of Harold and Tostig's men were not even wearing armour. The last thing they were expecting was an English attack.

But news of the Viking victory at Fulford had swiftly reached King Harold Godwinson. His response had been immediate. His men, having been on call all summer for an expected attack by William of Normandy, had recently been disbanded. Nevertheless, Harold was immediately able to summon another army; a testament to Anglo-Saxon military organisation and efficiency, helped by his forces possibly still being on high alert. Harold marched his army north, covering 200 miles in just six days. On arrival at Tadcaster, he learned that the enemy was at Stamford Bridge. He decided to launch a surprise attack.

Today Stamford Bridge is a large village on the outskirts of York. In 1066, it was essentially a crossing point over the river

Derwent, with no nearby dwellings as far as we know. The crossing most probably consisted of a wide wooden bridge on stone piles, a little further along the river from the eighteenth-century bridge in the village today. The sources of the time tell of how, from afar, the Norsemen saw sunlight glinting on the chain mail and shield bosses of the approaching army, and could not work out who might be coming. When they did realise, they would have been painfully aware of their huge disadvantage. The bulk of the Norse army was safely on the east side of the river, but a number were vulnerably on the west, right in the path of the enemy. And many of their fighting men were 10 miles away at Riccall, guarding the ships where they were moored.

King Harold of England at his coronation.

Hardrada sent word to Riccall for the rest of his men to make haste to Stamford Bridge, armed for battle.

But the Anglo-Saxons did not attack immediately. King Harold first rode across to his brother Tostig, to offer him peace. He also promised to return his former earldom of Northumbria to him, if only he would surrender. Tostig asked what his ally Harald Hardrada would receive, to which King Harold bluntly replied, 'Seven feet of ground, or as much more as he is taller than other men.' Tostig refused Harold's terms, unwilling to abandon Hardrada. The attempt at negotiating peace had failed.

The first fighting was on the west side of the bridge, as the English attacked the bewildered soldiers who were stranded there and desperately trying to get across the river to join the others.

The most famous part of the Stamford Bridge story occurs at this point, where a huge Viking axe-man stood on the bridge, and single-handedly fought off the English attackers, making it impossible for any of them to get past him. Every time a man approached, he was cut down by the axe. He was finally stopped by a warrior who floated under the bridge on a half-barrel and skewered him from below, a somewhat undignified ending for such a heroic character. The story, added to the *Anglo-Saxon Chronicle* 100 years after the event, may or may not be true, but it has been an enduring image, commemorated today in Stamford Bridge by the sign of the pub The Swordsman's Inn.

On the east side of the bridge, Hardrada's army set up a shield wall on higher ground. King Harold's warriors attacked, smashing at the shields with

Swordsman Inn sign, showing the famous Viking on the bridge, who killed all who attempted to pass until finally skewered from below.

axes, swords and spears. Eventually the Vikings were forced back on to flatter ground, and the English gained the upper hand. Here, the legendary Harald Hardrada met his end, killed with an arrow through his throat. As his men were pushed even further back, the fighting spread out over an area now known as the Battle Flats, which would have been a scene of carnage on the afternoon of 25 September in 1066. According to writer Orderic Vitalis, the battlefield was still strewn with human bones seventy years later. Later in the afternoon, reinforcements for the Vikings arrived from Riccall under Eystein Orri; the final part of the battle is known as 'Orri's storm'. The Vikings were losing, but Orri's men refused to surrender, fighting on to the death. Around this time, Tostig Godwinson was killed.

The English army pursued the remaining Vikings all the way back to

Battle of Stamford Bridge memorial.

their ships at Riccall, and even here the slaughter did not stop. It is thought that there could have been up to 4,000 bodies in the fields and marshes between Stamford Bridge and Riccall, and that Viking losses at Stamford Bridge may have been proportionally greater than the number of English lost at Hastings. In any case, out of the 300 Viking ships which initially invaded, only twenty-four were needed to take the surviving men home.

Although no evidence of the battle has ever been unearthed at Stamford Bridge, a number of skeletons have been found in the fields at Riccall, all

buried together miles from the nearest churchyard. Many bear marks and cuts consistent with battle wounds, and a recent investigation looking specifically at DNA found they were individuals of Norwegian ancestry. It is likely that these are the remains of some of Harald Hardrada's army, killed as they fled back to their ships.

King Harold scored a decisive victory at Stamford Bridge, effectively quashing the last Viking attempt at a full-scale invasion of England. However, three days later, on 28 September, William the Conqueror landed with his army on the south coast of England. Harold now had to march immediately back south with his battle-weary men, to meet the Normans at Hastings. On 14 October 1066, less than three weeks after Stamford Bridge, King Harold was defeated and killed at the Battle of Hastings, and the Anglo-Saxon era of British history was at an end. Had King Harold not had Hardrada to contend with, the outcome of Hastings and the subsequent course of history might have been very different.

WILLIAM NOT WELCOME

NORMANS WERE NOT WANTED IN THE NORTH

William the Conqueror might have won the battle of Hastings in 1066, but he had not yet won the country and certainly not the North. The chronicler Orderic Vitalis reports that 'York was seething with discontent.' And according to the *Anglo-Saxon Chronicle*, 'The king was informed that the people in the North had gathered together, and meant to make a stand against him if he came.'

Yet when William finally marched north with his army in 1068, the rebels seem to have decided it was futile to engage him in battle. The nearer the Conqueror got to York, the more he gave proof of his own ruthlessness and of his army's strength, building castles and laying waste to land as he went. The intimidation tactics worked, and William was able to enter York unopposed. The leading Yorkshire theigns (nobles) submitted to him, and he took hostages to guarantee their allegiance. But he did nothing to win their genuine support.

William built a castle in York from which to control the region. It was a wooden precursor of Clifford's Tower, on the site where the famous York landmark stands today. He then flooded the whole of the Coppergate area to create a moat. An entire 'scyra' (ward) of the town was lost, including two mills and 120 acres of land. William left a garrison of 500 knights in the castle, under the leadership of castellan Richard FitzRichard and Sheriff William Malet. It was a high number of men compared to other places, seeming to indicate William perceived a strong threat in York – and with good reason. The Northumbrians were far from happy and, as they had not been drawn into battle, their military strength remained intact.

In January 1069, still worried about the possibility of a northern uprising, William imposed a Norman earl on Northumbria – Robert de Comines. De Comines made his presence felt immediately, riding north to Durham with a force of 900 men, allowing them to wreak havoc as they went. In Durham, the rampage continued into the night as people were killed and the city plundered. The following morning, as soon as dawn broke, the Northumbrian forces retaliated. They burst into Durham, slaughtering Normans so that soon there were piles of corpses in the

Anglo-Saxons and Normans in battle (detail from the Bayeux tapestry).

streets. De Comines was among the dead. Encouraged by the success of the attack, the Northumbrians decided to march on York, appealing in advance to its people for help, and to King Swein Esrithson of Denmark for military support.

The Northumbrian Army stormed York, and captured the castle. Although the Normans tried to drive them off, they were hugely outnumbered and all were killed or taken prisoner. Castellan Richard FitzRichard was also killed, and the victorious Northumbrians sent word to Edgar the Aethling, a descendant of King Edward the Confessor, asking him to be their leader. This, however, turned out to be premature. Somehow, the Norman garrison had managed to send word to the king, who raced north and arrived unexpectedly in the city on 20 September 1069. William crushed the Northumbrian uprising, killing hundreds of men.

The *Anglo-Saxon Chronicle* tells us that, in his fury, William ravaged the city of York, and the Minster was 'made an object of scorn.' The Conqueror now built a second castle in York, on the opposite bank of the river Ouse (no longer standing today but still visible as a mound known as Baille Hill). In March he returned south, leaving William FitzOsbern in charge, a dour and ruthless man who had been responsible for the slaughter of a great number of the Northumbrians.

Then, in September 1069, a Danish army finally arrived in England in response to the Northumbrians' pleas for support. The Danes anchored their ships on the Humber, and were joined by many Anglo-Scandinavian leaders. Those leaders who had previously been enemies were prepared to overlook their differences and unite against the common foe. Nobility from the north included the House of Bambrugh, Thorbrand the Hold, and the supporters of St Cuthbert's men, all of whom resented Norman occupation of lands which had previously been theirs. They readied themselves for attack.

On 19 September, knowing that a strike was imminent, the Norman garrison at York set fire to the houses surrounding the two castles, to eliminate potential cover for their enemy. Unfortunately the fire spread and was soon out of control, burning down much of the town, including York Minster.

On 21 September the attack the Normans had anticipated was launched, but when the Danes and Northumbrians arrived in York they found the city gutted by fire. The Normans had been driven out of the castles by fire, and a reported 3,000 were slain, their corpses left for the wolves. Earl Waltheof, according to one saga, was the hero of the day: 'he single-handedly killed many Normans in the battle of York, cutting off their heads one by one as they entered the gate.'

It was an overwhelming victory for the Northumbrians, and for a short time there was a real possibility of a new Northumbrian kingdom emerging, under Edgar the Aethling. But the Danes turned out not to be a serious ally, in England mainly for the plunder rather than helping oust the Normans. The English hid, waiting to rendezvous with the Danes so they could meet William in battle. But by now the Danes were having a bad winter, with no real place to stay since York was uninhabitable. As the winter months progressed, many died of starvation. When William offered them a bribe to leave, they accepted gladly. York had been all but destroyed, and the chance of an independent Northumbria was lost for good.

ST CUTHBERT PROTECTS NORTHUMBRIA

After the death of Robert de Comines, William the Conqueror sent some of his men out into Northumbria to exact revenge. They rode from York as far as Northallerton, but here 'a great darkness' descended upon them. The men had most likely run into fog, but they became scared as there was a legend that St Cuthbert still acted to defend his land. The Normans decided it was unsafe to continue, and returned to York. St Cuthbert (c. 634-687) is still regarded as the patron saint of northern England.

St Cuthbert.

AD 1069–70

THE HARRYING
OF THE NORTH

BRUTAL VIOLENCE AND DEVASTATION

William the Conqueror was enraged by the Northumbrians' continued resistance. They had massacred his York garrison twice, set the Danes on him, and, humiliatingly, had caused his own men to burn down much of York. He returned to the north to implement a new and more effective weapon to enforce control: terror.

First, however, as a show of his power, William celebrated the third anniversary of his coronation, and the feast of Christmas in York. He wore his crown and royal regalia throughout, reminding the people that he did not merely possess military might: he was also their legitimate king, anointed to rule by God. The celebration presumably took place in what was left of York Minster which, according to the *Anglo-Saxon Chronicle*, was 'completely laid waste and burnt down'. It is odd and somehow unsettling to imagine William in his glittering crown and royal robes among the blackened ruins, making his presence and power felt.

The Conqueror and his men then set out to take revenge on the north.

The Danes were out of the way and the northern rebels had withdrawn to the moors, dales and forests. Parties of Norman knights now combed Yorkshire, rooting the rebels out from their dens for the slaughter. And it did not stop there. William intended to make sure the north of England would never again be able to either raise or sustain another army to oppose him. He systematically set about laying waste to the whole of the region.

The destruction began in the ancient heartlands of Northumbria, where William himself destroyed the church in Jarrow by fire. The harrying, as it came to be known, continued for almost an entire year, from February to December, covering around 1,000 square miles. The Normans devastated the north.

Not only were people killed, but also food supplies were burned. Crops were uprooted and torched, animals were slaughtered in the fields, and at Nantwich the salt works were destroyed, removing the means of preserving food for the winter months. All possible means of sustenance and even farming tools were destroyed.

Famine soon followed. The deaths from starvation continued for months. The eleventh-century writer, Simeon of

William commanding his knights.

Durham, tells us, 'there was such hunger that men ate the flesh of their own kind, of horses and dogs and cats. Others sold themselves into perpetual slavery that they might be able to sustain their miserable lives. It was horrible to look into the ruined farmyards and houses and see the human corpses dissolved into corruption, for there were none to bury them for all were gone either in flight, or cut down by the sword and famine. None dwelt there and travellers passed in great fear of wild beasts and savage robbers.'

People who managed to get away from the region arrived in other parts of England, seeking aid. The chronicler of far-away Evesham Abbey in Worcestershire recorded the arrival of large numbers of starving refugees from Yorkshire, some of whom died from eating too much too quickly.

The effects of the harrying were felt for years, and the Domesday Book, compiled almost twenty years later in 1086, bears testament to this. It contains records for all the towns and villages in the country, and many places in Yorkshire are recorded simply as 'waste'. There is also very little general information listed for some Yorkshire villages, probably because the people who could have provided it were no longer alive. In York, 540 tenements are described as 'waste' and 400 as partially wasted, possibly still as a result from the fire of 1069.

Apparently, William later regretted his actions in Northumbria. Oderic Vitalis recounts a speech he supposedly gave on his deathbed:

> I treated the native inhabitants of the kingdom with unreasonable severity, cruelly oppressed high and low, unjustly disinherited many, and caused the death of thousands by starvation and war, especially in Yorkshire ... I descended on the English of the north like a raging lion, and ordered that their homes and crops and furnishings should be burnt at once and their great flocks and herds of cattle and sheep slaughtered everywhere ... alas! (I) was the cruel murderer of many thousands, both young and old, of this fair people.

The scale of the human suffering caused by the harrying of the north was truly

William the Conqueror, dividing up England between his nobles.

certainly did not condone William's actions:

> My narrative has frequently had occasion to praise William, but for this act which condemned the innocent and guilty alike to die by slow starvation I cannot commend him. For when I think of helpless children, young men in the prime of life, and hoary greybeards perishing alike of hunger, I am so moved to pity that I would rather lament the grief and sufferings of the wretched people than make a vain attempt to flatter the perpetrator of such infamy. Moreover, I declare that assuredly such brutal slaughter cannot remain unpunished. For the almighty Judge watches over high and low alike; he will weigh the deeds of all in an even balance, and as a just avenger will punish wrongdoing, as the eternal law makes clear to all men.

shocking, even to people at the time who were used to a degree of barbarism as part and parcel of life. Oderic Vitalis

CLIFFORD'S TOWER

Clifford's Tower – or The King's Tower, as it was originally known – was once a forbidding and unwelcome sight in York. It was a symbol of Norman control and oppression, and a reminder to the people of their own powerlessness. William the Conqueror built 500 such towers during his brutal campaigns to subdue and control the country.

The original Norman King's Tower was burnt down in 1190, at the tragic massacre of 150 of York's Jews who had taken refuge there (see next chapter). A new wooden tower was rebuilt afterwards, but in the thirteenth century Henry III had it rebuilt in stone. It is not until the end of the sixteenth century that the first recorded use of the name 'Clifford's Tower' occurs. The Clifford family were hereditary constables of the tower, but it is unclear if the name actually refers to them. It could also refer to Roger de Clifford who was hanged at the tower in 1322 for opposing King Edward II.

MASSACRE AT CLIFFORD'S TOWER

YORK'S DARKEST DAY

The massacre of the Jews at Clifford's Tower is one of the most harrowing stories in the history of York. Today, the current tower is an iconic landmark often used to symbolise the city, and it is disturbing to remember that in 1190, the 150 men, women and children of York's Jewish community lived their last days in that very place, in misery and terror.

The chain of events began not in York, but in London, at the coronation of King Richard I in July 1189. The Jews had always had a special relationship with the king, dating from when they were first invited to England by William the Conqueror. Since Christians were forbidden to make a profit from money lending, which was condemned as the sin of usury, an arrangement was made for Jews to practise the occupation in England. Many money lenders made

Clifford's Tower.

SYMBOLIC FLOWERS

The daffodils on the motte of Clifford's Tower were planted in 1990 by English Heritage and the American Jewish Foundation as a symbolic reminder of the tragedy. The six petals represent the points on the Star of David. The flowers come into bloom every year in mid-March, the anniversary of the massacre.

fortunes, but they were also heavily taxed. In return, the Jews were afforded the king's protection. Under Henry II, they prospered and were well protected. But when Richard I came to the throne the country was in the grip of crusade fever and anti-Semitism was rife.

At Richard I's coronation banquet, a group of Jewish men arrived to pay their respects to him. Among them was Benedict, the wealthiest of the York Jews. The Jews' arrival caused outrage, and they were barred from entering the banquet. In the ensuing mob violence they were brutally attacked. Benedict was forced to convert to Christianity and he was also mortally wounded.

In the following months, with the new king away on a crusade, anti-Semitic riots spread across the country. In March 1190, a mob in York attempted to burn and loot Benedict's house, and his wife and children were killed. York's Jews feared for their lives. Under the leadership of Benedict's colleague Josce, they fled their homes and sought their right of royal protection from the constable at York Castle. To keep them safe, they were barricaded inside the keep. The looting in York continued, however, and the Jews in the tower lost confidence that the constable was doing anything to help them. Fearing that he would betray them, they refused to let him back in.

An angry mob soon surrounded the keep, and the constable appealed for help to John Marshall, the Sheriff of Yorkshire, who issued a command for the Jews to be ejected by force. The sheriff's county 'milites' arrived on the scene, unfortunately sending out the signal to the crowd that an attack on the Jews would have royal approval. The fire of the crowd's anti-Semitic fervour was further stoked by a group of local noblemen: Richard Malebisse, William Percy, Marmeduke Darrell and Philip de Fauconberg. All of them had incurred extensive debts to York's Jewish moneylenders, which they could not afford to repay. In the king's absence from the country, they had spotted an opportunity to erase their debts.

On Friday 16 March, siege engines were brought to the castle. The Jews were told that if they agreed to convert to Christianity they would be granted safe passage out of the tower – otherwise their safety could not be guaranteed. For the 150 people trapped inside, there was now a grim choice to make: forced conversion and probable slaughter at the hands of the mob, or they could take their own lives. Most opted for suicide.

Rabbi Yomtob of Joigny and Josce presided over the pact. The men first slit the throats of their wives and children, then Yomtob and Josce probably killed the men, before killing themselves. They had also set fire, at some point, to the wooden keep. At daybreak, those who had opted to face the crowd and had managed to survive the fire came out of the tower, appealing for Christian mercy in return for baptism. They did not receive it, and were massacred by the mob.

It was also a tragic ending for Benedict, who died from the wounds inflicted on him at Westminster. While on his deathbed he renounced his conversion to Christianity, but was still not permitted to have a Jewish burial. Nor was he allowed a Christian one.

After the murder of the Jews, Richard Malebisse seized the records of the nobles' debts from York Minster and burned them, so that they could not be transferred to the king. When Richard I learned of the massacre at York, it was seen as an affront to his honour, and a royal inquest was held. The city was heavily fined, but no individuals were ever punished.

CEMETERY UNDER THE CAR PARK

In 1984 archaeologists discovered the remains of a Jewish cemetery in Jewbury. It was in use from 1177 till the Jewish expulsion of 1290. No evidence was found for the remains of those who died in the Clifford's Tower massacre, but only 500 of the estimated 1,000 burials were excavated. The remaining 500 bodies lie undisturbed under what is now Sainsbury's car park.

Jewish cemetery memorial.

AD **1319**

THE WHITE BATTLE

MARAUDING SCOTS AND A VERY ODD BATTLE

In the late thirteenth century, King Edward I transformed York from a peaceful civilian town into a powerful centre of military operations. His first expedition, which set out from the city in the spring of 1296, was the beginning of what was to be 300 years of war with Scotland. And in 1319, an attempt by the Scots to attack York would result in what was probably one of the oddest battles ever fought.

York, with its defensive walls and relative proximity to Scotland, was the ideal choice for Edward I's military base. Size was another factor – it was already the second largest town in the country next to London, with an estimated 12,000 inhabitants. As the fighting continued, York became a rendezvous point for English armies on their way north, as well as a place for them to purchase provisions. Literally thousands of soldiers were passing through; it was a prosperous time for the town's merchants and innkeepers. Edward I's objective of becoming the king of the Scots as well as the English was never achieved, although he did gain the nickname 'the Hammer of the Scots'.

When Robert the Bruce became King of Scotland, the military threat to York increased hugely. Edward II was now King of England and, through necessity, he spent many of the early years of his reign in the city. But at the Battle of Bannockburn in 1314, Edward suffered a humiliating defeat. Bruce, on the other hand, had begun his rise to legendary status. The power balance had changed and suddenly England no longer looked so strong. Scottish raids into Yorkshire became a frequent occurrence, and were largely unchecked. On one occasion Ripon Cathedral was forced to pay 1,000 marks to avoid attack.

Battlefield at Myton-on-Swale.

Detail from the battlefield sign, showing Archbishop de Melton's army of clergy and farmers.

In 1319, a Scottish army set out towards York, led by the Earl of Moray and James the Black Douglas. Further north, Robert the Bruce had taken Berwick-upon-Tweed, and King Edward II was laying siege to the town with all the fighting men he could muster. As a diversion, and perhaps also because the opportunity presented itself, Bruce sent Moray and Douglas into Yorkshire to wreak havoc and to kidnap Queen Isabella, who was staying in York. But the Scots' armies' plans were leaked, and Isabella was quickly taken out of York to safety.

It was at this point that events took a rather bizarre turn. Not content with foiling the Scots' plans by conveying the Queen to safety, the Archbishop of York, William de Melton, decided he should set out after them to teach them a lesson. So on the eve of the feast of St Matthew, 20 September 1319, along with Lord Mayor of York Nicholas Fleming, the Archbishop raised an 'army' to go after the marauding Scots. There were very few professional soldiers around, as all were engaged in the siege at Berwick, but the Archbishop nevertheless managed to muster around 10,000 men from York

and the surrounding areas. His army consisted of tradesmen, merchants, farmers armed with rakes and hoes, and priests and monks clad in their Church vestments. One can only imagine the astonishment of the Scots when what must have been one of the strangest armies they had ever seen caught up with them at Myton-on-Swale, some 10 miles north of York.

The battle which ensued was not one of equals. The Scots' army consisted of battle-hardened veterans, led by experienced military commanders. Seeing that they were dealing with a very makeshift and inexperienced outfit, the Scots feigned a retreat, drawing the Archbishop's men towards them over a wooden bridge across the river Swale. Once the Yorkshire men had fallen into the trap, they suddenly found themselves blinded by smoke; the Scots had set fire to three haystacks and were advancing towards their quarry under the smoke's cover. The Scots charged, and what happened next was a massacre, the makeshift army from York cut down by swords and billhooks. There was no retreat back across the bridge, which was now blocked by the Scots, and many

YORK SAFE AGAIN FOR SCOTTISH ARCHERS

Until very recently, an archaic law was still in force which made it legal to kill a Scotsman within the city walls of York, providing he was carrying a bow and arrow. Modern-day Scottish archers visiting York can now relax, however, as the law was finally repealed in the 2012 Statute Law Bill.

Longbow archers.

threw themselves into the Swale in an attempt to escape. An estimated 1,000 men met their end through drowning that day. Finally, nightfall enabled the remaining Yorkshiremen to escape, but thousands had been slain in battle, hundreds of them priests. Sir Nicholas Fleming, in his seventh year as Mayor of York, was among the dead. He is the only Mayor of York ever to be killed in action. His body was brought back to York, and he was given a respectful burial in the church of St Wilfred. The little church at Myton-on-Swale had to deal with the burial of the rest of the corpses.

The Battle of Myton came to be known as the White Battle because of the many white vestments of the clergy on the battlefield, both before and after the fighting. The Scots jokingly referred to it as the Chapter of Myton, since the presence of the clergy presumably made it look like the meeting of a cathedral chapter.

The next king, Edward III, spent more time in York than either of his two predecessors, and for convenience transferred all the main government departments there from London. But even he did not fare well in battling the Scots. Eventually he abandoned them and turned his military attentions to France instead. From the 1330s onwards, the realm's defence against Scottish raids was provided further north, by the king's castles in Northumberland, the Percy family and the Bishop of Durham. Despite this, York continued to be seen as the centre of defence against the Scots until the late medieval period.

ARCHBISHOP SCROPE EXECUTED

AND HENRY IV PUNISHED WITH VILE AFFLICTION

On 8 June 1405, the Archbishop of York, Richard le Scrope, was led out of the city to be executed for treason. He was made to ride facing backwards on an unsaddled mule. To keep in good cheer, Scrope sang Psalm 17 and told the gathered crowd that he died for the laws and good government of England. Through his own choice, the Archbishop was hacked to death – beheaded by five blows of the executioner's blade, to signify the five wounds of Christ. But unluckily for King Henry IV, who had ordered Scrope's execution, the much revered Archbishop was about to prove even more trouble to him dead than he had done alive.

Richard le Scrope was the fourth son of Baron Scrope of Masham, an important Yorkshire magnate, and benefactor of the Minster. He was

Tomb of Archbishop Scrope in York Minster. (Reproduced by kind permission of the Chapter of York)

Henry IV.

highly educated, a graduate of arts at Oxford and of law at Cambridge, where he also became a doctor of civil and common law.

Scrope's rise to stardom in the Church was meteoric and he was enthroned as Archbishop of York in 1398. He soon became a favourite of King Richard II, a king who had a very close relationship with the city of York and who, some say, would have made York the capital city of the kingdom in preference to London had he survived the turbulent era in order to do so. But in 1399 Richard II was deposed by Henry of Bolingbroke, and was left to die in Pontefract Castle. Meanwhile, his rival became King Henry IV. Although Scrope was on the committee which accepted Richard II's surrender of the crown, his conscience must later have gotten the better of him, as he began to work against Henry IV.

In typical northern fashion, there was no mincing of words in the manifesto Scrope helped the Percy family to compose for their 1403 rebellion. Henry

IV was directly accused of the murder of Richard II:

> ...thou hast traitorously caused him (Richard II), without consent or judgement of the lordes of the realme, by the space of XV dayes and nightes (which is horrible among Christians to bee heard) to perish & bee murthered with hunger, thirst & cold, within the castle of Pomfrett, wherefore thou art perjured & false.

In 1405, the Archbishop openly joined the Percys in rebellion. He also preached rebellion to York from the pulpit of the Minster and had other Churchmen do the same around Yorkshire. On 27 May, clad in full armour, Scrope led the people of York in an armed insurrection against the first Lancastrian King. York rose willingly, perhaps through loyalty to the Archbishop and also to Richard II, a king close to their hearts. Scrope promised remission of sins for all killed in the battle.

Under the banner of the five wounds of Christ, 8,000 men from York and the surrounding countryside met on Shipton Moor. They were led by Archbishop Scrope, Earl Thomas Mowbray and Sir William Plumpton. The intention was to join forces with the Percys' men at Topcliffe, but before the meeting could take place they were intercepted by the Royalist army of Prince John of Lancaster and the Earl of Westmoreland.

The Royalists, outnumbered and wanting to avoid a battle, tricked Scrope into surrender. Westmoreland looked at Scrope's manifesto, pretended to agree with it, and suggested that together they decide how to get Henry IV to agree to the demands. Scrope was persuaded to disband his army. As soon as he had done so, he was arrested and taken to Pontefract Castle.

Henry IV arrived on the scene, and demanded that Scrope's crozier (staff) be siezed. Having already decided that the Archbishop was to be executed, he refused to see him, and set up a commission to have him tried at Bishopthorpe. The commission promptly pronounced Scrope, Mowbray and Plumpton guilty of treason, and sentenced them to death, despite Scrope's denial that they had ever intended to cause injury to the king.

At his execution in the barley fields of Clementhorpe nunnery, outside the walls of York, Scrope behaved like an exemplary martyr. He offered encouragement to his fellow victims, and he kissed and forgave his executioner. The brave but brutal manner by which he chose to die, with five blows of the axe, was not easy for those who witnessed it to forget.

After the execution, Mowbray and Plumpton's heads were spiked on Micklegate Bar. But as he was an Archbishop, Scrope's body was taken back to the Minster, where it was interred in the Lady Chapel, his severed head reverently placed between his left arm and his body. Almost immediately, to the dismay of Henry IV, the tomb became a place of pilgrimage. In fact, so many people poured in to pay their respects that a shrine had to be set up to hold the votive offerings they brought. Miracles were said to happen there, and there were calls for Scrope to be canonized.

While Archbishop Scrope grew in popularity after death, Henry IV's luck in life had run out. He was excommunicated by the Pope for the Archbishop's murder and was also stricken with a foul skin complaint which everyone believed – including Henry himself – was a direct result of having had Scrope executed. His affliction caused him to scream out that he was on fire, and pustules and tumours 'like teats' on his face left him completely disfigured.

Archbishop Scrope was never officially canonized, due both to Lancastrian hostility and the fact that he had rebelled against the crown, but locally he was regarded as a saint. The devotional cult which grew up around him flourished, and for at least the next 100 years his shrine was one of the holiest places in the north. Income generated by pilgrims also helped the Minster grow. Henry IV died of his vile affliction in 1413.

RICHARD OF YORK
GAVE BATTLE IN VAIN

AND HIS HEAD ENDED UP ON MICKLEGATE BAR

Richard, Duke of York, has been made famous to generations of English schoolchildren by the well-known mnemonic 'Richard Of York Gave Battle In Vain', in which the first letters of each word correspond to the colours of the rainbow. The man himself did indeed give battle in vain. He never succeeded in becoming King of England – and worse still, his head ended up on a spike on York's Micklegate Bar. So how did it all go so horribly wrong for the man made famous by the rainbow rhyme?

Life at least started out well for Richard Plantagenet. He was born into a branch of the royal family descended from Edward III, and came into so many inheritances that, by the age of twenty-one, he was the richest and most powerful magnate in the country. He owned land in Wales, in Ireland and in thirteen English counties. He owned castles in Ludlow, Fotheringay and London. And Richard married well, into the famous northern family the Nevilles, and had a stronger claim to the throne by royal descent than the current king.

But it was exactly this combination of power, wealth and royal lineage that made Richard a threatening figure to the Lancastrian king, Henry VI, and his entourage. Although Richard held various offices of state, he found himself the subject of constant criticisms and was frequently excluded at court.

The situation was aggravated by the fact that Henry VI was a weak king, surrounded by powerful magnates wrangling for power. His domineering wife, Margaret of Anjou, took an instant dislike to Richard. The feeling

King Henry VI and Margaret of Anjou, at their wedding.

THE WARS OF THE ROSES

The Wars of the Roses were a thirty year long civil war, in which the rival royal houses of Lancaster and York slaughtered one another for the crown of England. Over time, two roses have come to symbolise the two houses – white for York and red for Lancaster.

Both Lancaster and York were branches of the Plantagenet family, which had ruled England since 1154. It is sometimes mistakenly thought that the wars were about Yorkshire versus Lancashire, but the names only refer to the royal dynasties, not geographical areas. It was in fact more of a North-South divide. The Lancastrians were mainly men of the north, including Yorkshiremen and some Scots, whilst the Yorkists found their support mostly in southern England and Wales.

The York Rose. The white rose has been associated with the House of York since medieval times. It was not until the Victorian era that it began to be used as an emblem of York. In the twentieth century, this seems to have been generalised to the whole of Yorkshire.

was mutual. When Henry began to suffer from bouts of mental illness, during which he could neither speak nor recognise people, the wrangling for power at court escalated. Against this backdrop, Richard found allies willing to support him in his own bid for power. While there is nothing to suggest that he had designs on the crown from the very beginning, it seems as though frustration drove him to pursue it as the king became increasingly incapable of ruling.

A first armed conflict took place at St Albans in 1455 – the Wars of the Roses had begun. More battles were fought, and the Yorkists were even banished from the country for a while. But in 1459 they were back, and Richard made a bold bid for the throne, famously putting his hand on it as a claim, in front

of a shocked court. Although he did not succeed, he was officially recognised by Parliament as Henry VI's successor, in preference to Henry's own young son. Margaret of Anjou and the Lancastrian nobles were furious. They managed to

Sandal Castle, Wakefield, one of the many properties of Richard, Duke of York.

Richard of York's head (don't worry – it's a replica) at Micklegate Bar Museum. (By kind permission of Micklegate Bar Museum and the York Archaeological Trust)

troops, Richard rode out at the head of his men on to Wakefield Green to face the Lancastrian army, along with his seventeen-year-old son Edmund, Duke of Rutland. Why Richard left the castle to fight against an army which so severely outnumbered his own is a much debated mystery, but it seems he was lured out by traitors who led him to believe he would be facing a much smaller force.

Not only were the Yorkists outnumbered, but they were also skilfully out-manoeuvred. No sooner had Richard advanced than the Lancastrians closed in behind him as well as in front. He was trapped 'like a fish in a net or a deer in a buckstall'. And in the middle of the fighting, which was later to become known as the Battle of Wakefield, Richard was dragged from his horse and slain. His son Edmund was also killed, with a dagger through the heart, by the Lancastrian Lord Clifford, in revenge for the Duke of York's murder of his own father.

amass a huge force in the north, to strike at Richard. Richard rode north to his property Sandal Castle, near Wakefield, and it was while he was here, building an army of his own, that his downfall came.

On 30 December 1460, despite still being in the process of mustering

Later, when the battle was over, Lancastrian soldiers are said to have propped the Duke of York's body up against an ant-hill, put a crown made of reeds on his head, and pretended to bow to him, saying, 'Hail, king without

THE HOUSE OF YORK

The Dukedom of York was created by King Richard II and given to Edmund, the first Duke of York, in 1385. Edmund had led an army on an expedition to Scotland, and they had camped at York on the way. The naming of the Dukedom could have been to show gratitude to York for this, or because of Richard II's close connection with the city.

ANOTHER UNFORTUNATE DUKE OF YORK

Edward of Norwich was the second Duke of York, uncle of Richard. After death, his body met with an even more revolting fate than having its head spiked on Micklegate Bar. Edward died at the Battle of Agincourt. He was very overweight and is thought to have suffered a heart attack, or suffocated to death in his armour. In order to transport his rather large corpse back to England more easily, he was put in a huge cooking pot overnight until his flesh had boiled away. Just his bones were taken back home for burial.

a kingdom!' Clifford ordered Richard's body to be decapitated, along with that of Edmund, and their heads were spiked on lances and taken to be displayed on Micklegate Bar. Richard was decorated with a paper crown. In Shakespeare's play *Henry VI*, Margaret of Anjou orders York's head to be put on the Bar, 'so that York will overlook the town of York'.

With the death of Richard, Duke of York, the Wars of the Roses could have ended. But Richard's kinsfolk were not willing to abandon the cause, nor let his and Edmund's murders go without vengeance. Much more blood was yet to be spilled.

Micklegate Bar, York's main gateway, was once adorned with severed heads – which meant rotting bits fell off onto the pedestrians below. The last heads spiked here were in 1746 but were stolen a few years later and never recovered.

TOWTON

THE BLOODIEST BATTLE FOUGHT ON BRITISH SOIL

The Battle of Towton, fought just 12 miles south-west of York, was one of the biggest, bloodiest and most horrific battles ever fought in Britain. It was not just the scale of the clash, the staggering numbers of men involved, or that the slaughter lasted literally from morning until night which made Towton so horrific. It was also the brutality of the rout which ended it, turning the battle into a massacre. Edward, son of the recently decapitated Duke of York, would allow no mercy to be shown to the Lancastrians.

On the morning of 29 March 1461, the two armies faced each other across meadows near the village of Towton. The Yorkists were led by Edward of March, the nineteen-year-old son of the late Duke of York. He intended to avenge his father, brother and uncle, killed at the Battle of Wakefield, whose heads were impaled on Micklegate Bar. Although young in years, Edward was strong in both character and appearance, and he inspired confidence in his men. The Lancastrians, who fought for King Henry IV, were led by the Duke of Somerset. It is thought that, altogether,

there were as many as 75,000 men on the field.

It was a bitter day; a thick blizzard had been blowing since dawn. The Lancastrians, on the higher ground, appeared to have the initial advantage, but as the first volleys of arrows were fired by the archers it became clear that the wind was in favour of the Yorkists.

Edward of March was just nineteen when he led the Yorkists at Towton, to avenge the deaths of his father, brother and uncle.

Each time the Yorkists' arrows arced upwards, turning the sky dark, they made their deadly descent straight into the enemy ranks, causing hundreds of Lancastrians to fall. As well as arrows, thick snow was blowing straight at the Lancastrians, making it hard for them to see the descending missiles, or even the enemy. And each time the Lancastrian archers fired up into the wind, their arrows fell short of the Yorkist lines; the Yorkists were even collecting them up in their thousands, and firing them back. When the Lancastrians realised what was happening, they had no choice but to charge across the field, still under constant fire, to engage in hand-to-hand combat.

The fighting was vicious, and lasted for 10 hours. As men hacked at one another, bodies began to pile up on the battlefield, and the snow became red with blood. Chronicler Jean de Wavrin wrote: 'There was great slaughter that day at Towton, and for a long time, no-one could see which side could gain the victory, so furious was the fighting.'

As dusk fell, however, Yorkist re-enforcements arrived, and the Lancastrians were pushed back on the western side of the meadows. Realising they were losing, the Lancastrians began to drop weapons and run for their lives. There was a steep hill on this part of the battlefield, and many men tried to escape down it, discarding their armour and whatever else they could on the way. At the bottom of the hill, the escape route was blocked by Cock Beck which had risen and was flooding. Many men skidded down the hill to escape, but were hacked to death by pursuing Yorkists. Others died of

Wars of the Roses battle scene, showing an older Edward as the crowned man on the left.

hypothermia in the freezing waters. This part of the battlefield became known as bloody meadow, and is just one of the places mass slaughter was occurring in the rout.

Hundreds of men tried to escape across a bridge over the flooded river, and a heavy battle broke out upon it as the Lancastrians tried to block their exit. The bridge, which could not support the weight of so many, cracked and broke, plunging all into the water and crushing or suffocating others. It is said that Cock Beck ran red with blood all the way to the River Wharfe.

The number of dead at Towton is thought to be a staggering 28,000. The corpses were stripped and were buried in huge mass graves on the field.

Edward of March was victorious. The morning after the battle, he rode into York in solemn procession through Micklegate Bar. The three rotting heads of his father, brother and uncle were still

Towton memorial (© Alison Clayton).

on display on top and Edward had them immediately removed. He ordered them to be decently buried, along with the corresponding bodies. Later in the week, heads of executed Lancastrians would adorn Micklegate Bar in their place.

Within three months, Edward was crowned King of England, becoming Edward IV. But this horrific battle did not bring peace. The Wars of the Roses were to continue for twenty more years.

AN AGE OF CHIVALRY?

Our image of medieval warfare is often a romantic one, involving chivalrous behaviour, and knights in shining armour. But evidence unearthed in a recently excavated mass grave near the battlefield at Towton shows how brutal the fighting actually was. The grave contained the bodies of thirty-seven men and boys. Aged between sixteen and fifty, their most common cause of death was a blade wound from a sword, dagger or battle axe. Many had sustained repeated head injuries, as though they had been mercilessly attacked while on the ground, by an assailant wielding a poleaxe or horseman's hammer. Their heads were unprotected, and their arms and hands had sustained cuts as they tried to protect themselves. Some of the skulls show repeated shallow cuts to the ears and face, probably deliberate mutilation. These unfortunate men were most likely Lancastrians caught in the rout at the end of the battle.

Knight in armour.

22 AUGUST 1485

THE DEATH OF RICHARD III

THE BRUTAL TREATMENT OF YORK'S MUCH LOVED KING

On 22 August 1485, Richard III was brutally slain at the Battle of Bosworth Field in Leicestershire. He was thirty-two years old and the last King of England to die in battle. The loss of a monarch who favoured York in the way Richard did was a huge blow for the city. The day after his death, it was recorded in the council minutes: 'King Richard, late mercifully reigning upon us ... was piteously slain and murdered, to the great heaviness of this city.' Two weeks later, the council referred to him as 'the most famous prince of blessed memory'.

Richard's relationship with the city of York went back a long way. He had first begun visiting while he was in his teens, and would either stay at the Augustinian Friary near the Guildhall, or at the Earl of Warwick's townhouse on Walmgate. Later, when Richard visited York in 1483, along with his wife Anne, he was given a magnificent reception as the new king. The celebrations were so impressive that some thought there had been a second coronation in York. In September of the same year, Richard's son Edward was invested as Prince of Wales at York Minster, and the royal family stayed in the city for three weeks. King Richard returned several times.

It is interesting that whenever Richard did visit, he was careful to develop good relations with the city council of York, and the Minster clergy. The main reason for this is thought to be that he planned to be buried in York. He certainly planned to have a huge chantry chapel attached to the Minster, attended by 100 chaplains, which was most likely intended to serve as his mausoleum.

Richard III had a strong following across the north of England. During the

Richard III.

THE GRIM FACTS OF RICHARD III'S DEATH

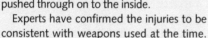

In 2012, the discovery of Richard III's remains under a Leicester car park enabled archaeologists to reconstruct the final moments of the king's life at Bosworth Field. Ten separate injuries were visible on the skeleton, eight of which were on the skull. The largest, most damaging injury was at the back of the head, where a section of the skull was sliced off, probably with a long pole weapon such as a halberd. On the other side, a blade had been forced deep into the head and, on top, a chunk had been taken out, with two flaps of bone pushed through on to the inside.

Skull of Richard III, discovered in 2012 in a Leicester car park. (© and with kind permission of the University of Leicester)

Experts have confirmed the injuries to be consistent with weapons used at the time. Long pole weapons such as billhooks and halberds could also be used to open up or prize off armour. Richard III's head injuries seem to have been inflicted once his helmet was off, the one on top of his head most likely caused by a dagger.

Some of the injuries on other parts of Richard III's body, such as his ribs, could only have been caused once his armour was completely off, and have been interpreted as 'humiliation injuries' inflicted after death. A particularly brutal injury to the pelvis, consistent with a blade wound inflicted from behind in an upward direction, suggests that Richard's body was stabbed through the buttocks as it lay over the horse carrying it to Leicester, in a symbolic act of humiliation.

Richard III window, York Minster. It shows Richard's coat of arms with two white boars and his motto 'loyaulte me lie' (loyalty binds me). (Reproduced by kind permission of the Chapter of York)

reign of his brother Edward IV, he had been Governor of the North, and had managed the northern political scene well. He had even led the north in battle, succeeding in recapturing Berwick from the Scots in 1482. After his marriage to Anne Neville, he was usually at one or other of his Yorkshire power bases, Middleham Castle in Wensleydale or Sherrif Hutton, 8 miles north-east of York.

But on a summer's day in 1485, the close relationship between the monarch and the city of York was brought to a swift and bloody end at Bosworth.

Richard's opponent was Henry Tudor, a Lancastrian who had been in exile in France for the past fourteen years, and had now returned with French mercenaries and family allies from Wales to challenge the king for the throne.

The battle had begun with fierce hand-to-hand fighting, which did not go well for the Yorkists. But when spies informed Richard that Henry Tudor was nearby, he decided that a quick way to end matters would be to kill Tudor in person.

Richard led his loyal household knights in a charge straight at Henry Tudor. He personally killed several men, and knocked down Henry's standard bearer. But the experienced French mercenaries served Tudor well, and their pikemen were able to break up the charge. Unfortunately for Richard, his horse became stuck in a marsh, which was the beginning of the end. The sources tell us that 'unhorsed and overpowered, the king was hacked to death by Welsh soldiers.' Richard's dead body was stripped and thrown across the back of a horse. It was then taken to Leicester, where it was put on public display for three days. The news of Richard's death was carried swiftly back to York. The city, struggling against the plague and in a serious financial slump, was to miss the patronage of its generous benefactor and *dominus specialissimus* – most special of all lords.

RICHARD III: MURDEROUS VILLAIN?

The popular image of Richard III has long been that of an evil murderer, as portrayed by the plays of Shakespeare. Influenced by the Tudor propaganda of his time, Shakespeare's Richard III was a 'crook back' (hunchback) with a withered arm, who murdered King Henry VI, his own brother the Duke of Clarence, and even his wife in order to marry his niece. Most famously, Shakespeare's Richard also murdered his two nephews in the Tower of London.

Although there is no conclusive evidence, it is definitely possible that the real Richard could have had his two nephews murdered. He certainly shocked the country when, having previously been accepting of his nephew's right to the throne, he suddenly had the princes incarcerated in the Tower of London and proclaimed himself king. In York's Richard III museum, visitors are presented with the evidence for and against his guilt, and are invited to make up their own minds. Interestingly, the recent discovery of Richard III's remains has confirmed that the king suffered from scoliosis, a condition resulting in curvature of the spine. However, the withered arm of Shakespeare's Richard appears to have been a myth.

12 JULY 1537

ROBERT ASKE
HUNG IN CHAINS

YORK PUNISHED FOR REBELLION WITH A GRUESOME SPECTACLE

One of the cruellest executions to take place in York was that of Robert Aske. He was 'hung in chains' on a specially erected scaffold outside Clifford's Tower and left to die an agonising death. The point was not just to punish Aske but the entire city for rebellion against Henry VIII. Aske's decaying corpse, chained inside a gibbet, was a reminder of the fate which awaited would-be rebels. All over the North of England, others who had rebelled with Aske were executed in the same way, their communities similarly punished by the same barbaric spectacle in prominent public places.

The rebellion led by Robert Aske was known as the Pilgrimage of Grace. It began as a small-scale local uprising in the town of Beverley, against political and religious changes made by Henry VIII. Aske, a young lawyer with a talent for leadership, was the one who turned the rising into a rebellion. Soon, almost all of the north of England was up in arms against the king's religious reforms. It was a close call for Henry VIII and his chief henchman Thomas Cromwell; they came very close to losing control of the region.

One of the first acts of the rebellion, whose leaders wanted to keep as peaceful as possible, was to march on York in groups gathered around the crosses of their local parish churches. On 16 October 1536, the rebels arrived at the city gates and were allowed to enter, provided no harm was done to anyone and all food was paid for. Aske and the other leaders went to the Minster for a celebratory mass and, in the house of one of the city aldermen, Aske composed an oath to be sworn by all the gentry in his army and throughout the north. He also

Henry VIII, who had Aske sentenced to death.

HANGING IN CHAINS

A French visitor to England in the eighteenth century, Cesar de Saussure, described the process of 'hanging in chains' as it was practised around 200 years after the execution of Aske:

> There is no other form of execution but hanging; it is thought that the taking of life is sufficient punishment for any crime without worse torture. After hanging murderers are, however, punished in a particular fashion. They are first hung on the common gibbet, their bodies are then covered with tallow and fat substances, over this is placed a tarred shirt fastened down with iron bands, and the bodies are hung with chains to the gibbet, which is erected on the spot, or as near as possible to the place where the crime was committed, and there it hangs till it falls to dust. This is what is called in this country 'to hang in chains.'

A gibbet, in which victims would be 'hung in chains' (© Tony Avon).

In Tudor times, however, people were often hung in the gibbet while still alive and left to starve to death. The bodies were not allowed to be taken down for burial, and were left in the gibbet to rot. The gibbet's design ensured that the putrefying body stayed upright, and did not fall apart.

One of the last cases of live gibbeting occurred in the seventeenth century, on the moors behind Chatsworth House. The man was a tramp who had murdered a woman for refusing him food; he killed her by pouring boiling fat down her throat. Screams from the moors distressed the Duke of Devonshire to the extent that he personally campaigned to end live gibbeting in Derbyshire.

posted an order on the Minster doors, demanding the monks and nuns recently dismissed from religious houses to return. The allegiance of other Yorkshire towns was then sought. In some places aldermen were even waiting to welcome in the rebels' representatives, and convey them to an audience with the mayor.

The ready support is perhaps not surprising. There was widespread anger throughout Yorkshire at Henry's betrayal of the 'old' religion, and the split of the English Church from Rome. Thomas Cromwell, whose commissioners had begun to tour the country, dissolving monasteries and seizing treasures, was a hated figure. Not only did the Dissolution involve the closing of churches, but also of charitable institutions run by the

Church, such as hospitals for the poor who had no other means of assistance.

The Pilgrimage of Grace soon had around 30,000 followers. The rebels were disciplined and organised, and easily succeeded in capturing Pontefract Castle. When Henry sent out 4,000 mercenaries against them, under the command of the Duke of Norfolk, the rebels could have easily overcome them. But they did not. Norfolk knew he could not win a battle of arms, and instead, on 27 October at Doncaster Bridge, he negotiated a truce with Aske. On 6 December, Norfolk promised a royal pardon from the king, and agreed that many of the rebels' demands would be met. Eventually, after a lot of deliberation, the Pilgrimage of Grace was disbanded.

However, not long afterwards there were further rebellions in Cumberland and Westmorland, unauthorised by Aske. Henry used the opportunity to go back on his promise and crush the rebels completely. He ordered that the leaders of the Pilgrimage, including Robert Aske, be hunted down and be executed as traitors. In a letter to the Duke of Norfolk, the king said:

> Our pleasure is, that … you shall … cause such dreadful execution to be done upon a good number of the inhabitants of every town, village, and hamlet, that have offended in this rebellion, as well by the hanging them up in trees, as by the quartering of them and the setting of their heads and quarters in every town, great and small, and in all such other places, as they may be a fearful spectacle to all other hereafter, that would practice any like mater.

In the event, it seems that the seventy-four rebels selected by the Duke of Norfolk for execution were not hanged, drawn and quartered as Henry had wished. In a letter to Thomas Cromwell, Norfolk states that 'all in this shire were hung in chains'.

Henry now saw that he needed to take a much firmer hand with the north, and he set about the Dissolution of the Monasteries there with renewed vigour.

YORK IN THE DISSOLUTION

HENRY VIII PILLAGES THE CITY

Medieval York was an architecturally magnificent city. Its pinnacles, spires, guild halls, churches and almshouses formed a scene we can only now imagine. It was a scene which, between the years 1536 and 1540, was going to be forcefully and abruptly smashed down, along with the way of life which accompanied it. Henry VIII had begun his Dissolution of the Monasteries, and York had more to lose than most cities.

York's cathedral was the Minster, opposite which stood another building of similar grandeur and size: the Abbey of St Mary. York had priories, a nunnery, the Hospital of St Leonard, four friaries and no less than forty parish churches. In addition, thirty monasteries throughout Yorkshire had a base within the walls of York. And all of these religious institutions were busy, thriving places which depended on local labour and food provided by the city. Craftsmen in York supplied the Church with ornaments and vestments, and a printing press was set up at the beginning of the century to cater for the Church's printed matter requirements. The institution of the Church was the very fabric of the city, the structure around which everything else functioned. But it was unfortunately

---

YORK FORCED TO GROVEL BEFORE THE KING

In 1541, Henry VIII visited York to make the city grovel before him after its part in the Pilgrimage of Grace. Obediently, on 15 September 1541, at Fulford Cross, the mayor, aldermen and councillors, along with a crowd of commoners, gathered to meet Henry and his new bride Catherine Howard. The entire crowd knelt before the king and the recorder gave a long speech in which he confessed their 'most odious offence of treacherous rebellion'. They affirmed their regret 'from the bottoms of our stomachs' and renewed their pledge to serve the king. Henry was presented with silver cups containing £100 for him, and £40 for the queen.

ENCLOSURE AND CURSES

Another source of tension in Tudor York was the forced enclosure of land which had once been open for public use. It left local smallholders with nowhere for their animals to roam and graze. In May 1536 the commoners protested against enclosures on the Knavesmire, pointing out that their MP had said an Act of Parliament forbid it. The only result was that two citizens' wives were carted around York for three days, as it was alleged they had put a curse on the mayor and council for enclosing the common land.

a very rich fabric, and Henry intended to grab that wealth for himself.

The first stage in the Dissolution was the Act of Supremacy, passed in 1534, which made the king the Supreme Head of the Church and separated the Church in England from the authority of the Pope. In 1536, Henry's Church commissioners reached York, to assess how much the city's religious foundations were worth, and to find evidence of 'manifest sin, vicious, carnal and abominable living'. They immediately published a damaging report which resulted in Parliament passing an Act to close down religious houses worth less than £200 a year. As a result, in the summer of 1536,

Soldiers of Henry VIII.

Clementhorpe Nunnery and Holy Trinity Priory in Micklegate were suppressed.

In York there was tension and rioting, and in October 1536 Robert Aske led the Pilgrimage of Grace (see previous chapter) resulting in his execution the following July, as a punishment to the whole community for its rebellion. The Dissolution continued with a vengeance, and York's surviving religious houses were forced to submit to the crown as 'voluntary surrenders'. In November 1538, the Gilbertine Priory in Fishergate was the first. Then, in December, the Benedictine Priory of the Holy Trinity went through its second and final Dissolution. Just before Christmas, the next casualties were York's four friaries: the Dominicans on Toft Green, the Franciscans by the Castle, the Augustinians near the Guildhall and the Carmelites north of Fossgate. Then finally, in late 1539, the two richest and most important of York's religious foundations fell: the Abbey of St Mary, and the hospital of St Leonard. Unpopular locally, there may not have been many tears shed over the closure of the abbey – but the hospital was a different story.

Ruins of St Mary's Abbey.

St Leonard's was York's main hospital, and one of the biggest in the country. It cared not only for the sick, but also looked after orphans, the elderly and the destitute. Wealthy donors donated beds so the poor could be treated free of charge. The loss of St Leonard's hospital was tragic, and there was now little medical provision in York for the poor.

Many other smaller benefits which came with the religious institutions were also now lost to York. They included a boarding house, run by St Mary's Abbey, for fifty poor scholars at the Minster school, and a grammar school run by St Leonard's. There were probably hundreds out of work too, as the monasteries had employed servants from York and beyond, in addition to those local craftsmen regularly employed to provide goods and services. The religious establishments owned other properties in York besides their precincts, and these all came on the market for sale in

a very short period of time. It would take almost a generation for all the property to be redistributed.

York took on a dilapidated look, according to contemporary reports. Buildings were left without a purpose, and began to fall into ruin. They were pillaged for the lead from their roofs and stone for mending other buildings around the town. The only survivor was the nave of Holy Trinity church, as parishioners had established a right to worship there before the Reformation.

Just as brutal as the effects on the material fabric of the city were those on the community. Nuns and monks expecting to be in their religious orders for life had been cast out of their houses, the foundations on which their religious lives had been built. Some went on to work in other churches in the city, where they were a persistent thorn in Henry's side, resisting his changes at a fundamental level.

THE PRESSING OF MARGARET CLITHEROW

A BARBARIC EXECUTION ON OUSE BRIDGE

Of the many executions which took place in York throughout history, there is perhaps none that horrified the community so much as that of Margaret Clitherow. Not only was the method of execution barbaric, but the victim was a local woman well-known in York for her acts of good will, who faced her fate with bravery.

At eight o'clock in the morning, on Friday, 25 March 1586, the sheriffs came for her. Margaret Clitherow had decorated her hair with new ribbon, in much the same way she would have done on her wedding day fifteen years before, and over her arm she carried a short white linen habit she had sewn for the occasion. It was only 6 or 7 yards down Ouse Bridge, from the prison where she had spent the night to the toll booth where she was to be executed, but to the two city sheriffs, Gibson and Fawcett, the walk must have seemed uncomfortably long. 'Come away, Mrs Clitherow,' said Fawcett, trying to hurry her when she stopped to give alms to beggars on the bridge. 'Good Master Sheriff,' she replied, 'let me deal my poor alms before I now go, for my time is but short.' By the time Margaret knelt to pray before the sentence was to be carried out, Sheriff Gibson was openly weeping.

Margaret had lived all of her thirty-three years in York. She was brought up in a public house on Walmgate and both her father and later her step-father were respected community figures. She married the Shambles butcher John Clitherow at the age of fifteen, and at eighteen she converted to the Catholic faith. John did not convert, but was supportive of his wife's faith. Yorkshire Catholic Thomas Percy, Earl of Northumberland, was beheaded within 100 yards of Margaret's home in 1572. It is likely the moving speech he made before his death played a part in her conversion.

Although she was brought up as a Protestant, Margaret would have just remembered the times when 'the old religion' could be practised more freely and her father, a wax chandler, supplied candles to the church. The north of England had deep Catholic roots, but Queen Elizabeth I, who came to power just two years after Margaret was born, had brought in a series of increasingly punitive laws against Catholics.

Margaret was soon an active member of York's small but well-respected Catholic community. Mass was held in her home and she actively sought to bring others back to the Catholic faith. She also sheltered Catholic priests. Margaret was imprisoned three times prior to her final arrest, for failure to attend her local parish church. On the third occasion, she was in York Castle Prison for twenty months. Then, in 1585, an Act was passed which made sheltering a priest a felony, punishable by death. Margaret's house was searched and a young boy who was there to receive schooling was frightened by the soldiers. He showed them where the priests were hidden and Margaret was arrested and brought before the Assizes.

In court, Margaret was unable to plead guilty, as she believed she had done nothing wrong. And if she had pleaded not guilty, her family, including her children, would most likely have been tortured to obtain evidence against her. Therefore, she refused to plead at all. The sentence for this was as archaic as it was barbaric: *peine forte et dure*, a procedure in which a wooden door was laid on top of the victim, and weights were piled on top until the victim either uttered a plea or was crushed to death. But Margaret was resolute in her choice.

Ouse Bridge in 1856 looked very different from the wide, open bridge of today. It had various houses and buildings on both sides all the way along it. It was in this setting that the two Sheriffs marched Margaret Clitherow to the toll booth on the morning of her execution. Along with the sheriffs there were four constables charged with carrying out the execution, but they had hired a band of desperate beggars to do the dirty work. Various officials were also present, along with some women who helped Margaret change into her habit. The sentence had called for her to be

naked at her execution, but Margaret had made herself the short white garment, which covered her upper half and left her legs bare, to preserve her modesty as far as possible. She had even sewn strings to the sleeves, so that her arms could be tied in the same outstretched position as Christ on the cross.

At nine o'clock that morning, in the toll booth where she was to be executed, Margaret said her prayers. She prayed out loud for the Catholic church, the Pope and cardinals and the Catholic priests. Then she prayed that Elizabeth I should turn to the Catholic faith. Sheriff Fawcett said, 'Mrs Clitherow, you must remember and confess that you die for treason.' She answered, 'No, no, Mr Sheriff, I die for the love of my Lord Jesu.'

Margaret was made to lie on the floor of the toll booth and her face was covered with a handkerchief. Her hands were tied to two posts with the strings she had sewn, and a door was placed on top of her. A sharp stone 'as much as a man's fist' was placed under her back, and then the beggars began their work of piling on the weight. The last words she was heard to speak were 'Jesu! Jesu! Jesu! Have mercy upon me!' Eventually her ribs were broken, and burst out of her skin. Around 700lb in weight had been laid upon her. It took Margaret a quarter of an hour to die, and her body was left in the press for a further six hours.

The pressing of Margaret Clitherow was a cruel and horrific event which deeply marked the community in York. Today Margaret is recognised as a saint by the Catholic church, and there is a shrine dedicated to her in the Shambles.

THE PLAGUE IN YORK

'WHEN NATURE SICKENED AND EACH GALE WAS DEATH'

In May 1604 the most feared disease on earth entered York. In medieval times it had been known as the Pestilence. In the seventeenth century, it was the Black Death. Today, we know it as the Bubonic Plague, a name which still conjures all the mystery and horror associated with the deadly affliction.

The plague was a cruel and miserable illness, made worse by people not knowing what caused it, or how it was transmitted. Victims first fell ill with a flu-like fever, and soon began vomiting. Next, swellings or buboes appeared in their necks, armpits and groin, filled with pus and blood. On the skin, internal haemorrhaging produced purple and black blotches – hence the name, the 'Black Death'. At this stage, death came quickly with a pneumonia-like flooding of the lungs. As well as the vile and alarming symptoms, the rapid progression of the disease was an equal part of the horror, with sufferers usually dying just a few days after first falling sick.

By June 1604, seventeen households in York were known to be infected. The council set up plague lodges outside the city walls for those who were ill, and began to slaughter cats and dogs in the streets in case they were carrying the infection. But the plague proved impossible to control and councillors, the very people who were supposed to be helping with measures to contain it, began to flee the city in fear for their lives. The plague, which had started on the west bank of the river, soon spread throughout the city among poor and wealthy alike, until all of York's parishes were affected.

The burial register of St Olave's church, just outside the city walls, records that between August and December 'people dyed so fast that they

Plague sufferers.

PLAGUE DOCTORS

The plague doctor had the grim task of visiting sufferers to confirm whether or not they had the disease. They were not usually real doctors, but volunteers, well-paid by the cities which employed them for braving the very real risks of infection and death. A bird-like mask was worn by the 'doctors' as it was thought that birds spread the disease, and that wearing a bird mask could draw it back out of the patient. The beak of the mask was filled with herbs and spices to protect the wearer from the smell of sickness, also thought to spread the plague.

Plague doctor.

could not be well remembered.' Holy Trinity Goodramgate, just one of York's parish churches, records fifty-one burials for the month of September. Its records show whole households wiped out at a time.

With deaths on this scale, burying the bodies became a problem and could result in piles of rotting corpses waiting for disposal. Evidence has been found in London that bodies were already decomposed by the time they were buried in mass graves. In medieval Italy, dogs were reportedly running around carrying human arms and legs. We do not know what the situation was in York, but burying so many bodies would have been an immense challenge in all parishes.

As well as its devastating physical effects, the plague also affected the way people behaved towards each other. People were dying by the dozen, and it

was impossible for those left living to know how to react and cope. No-one knew how to make it stop. People could be unspeakably cruel, leaving others to die in boarded up houses. Families and friends shunned one another, avoiding the sick and everything to do with them.

It was not until the coming of the winter months that the disease eventually died down, and the last recorded plague burial was at All Saints' Pavement in April 1605.

Although the plague had visited York many times before, its 1604 visitation was one of the most deadly, wiping out an entire third of the city's population: over the summer and autumn of that year, there were an estimated 3,514 deaths.

Despite the huge death toll, however, the city recovered quickly. People flocked into York from the surrounding areas, as there was work to be had and accommodation vacant. Young people were able to find employment and embark upon prosperous lives. The after-effects of an outbreak of plague were that there was more of everything to go round for those left behind.

Although the disease broke out again in 1631, this time it was successfully contained in the parish of St Lawrence, outside the walls to the east of the city. The measures implemented to do so, however, were drastic ones, with the residents of Walmgate 'shutt up in their own severall houses and their back door lock upp or nayled upp and their fore doors also lock upp on the day'.

The threat of plague was in fact present for much of history, and people consequently lived their lives in very uncertain conditions. It was not until the end of the nineteenth century that the cause of the plague was finally discovered. Through the unimaginably disgusting process of cutting buboes off the corpses of victims and dissecting them, a Swiss scientist called Alexandre Yersin found that they contained a thick fluid, full of bacteria: *Yersinia pestis*. Within a short space of time, the bacteria's method of transmission was also discovered by one of Yersin's students. *Yersinia pestis* was carried by fleas, which lived on rats, and it was bites from these fleas which were the cause of the disease's transmission to humans. Plague does still occur in some part of the world today, but it can be successfully treated with antibiotics.

GUY FAWKES

THE GUNPOWDER PLOTTER FROM YORK

All over England, usually on the Saturday closest to 5 November, people celebrate Bonfire Night by attending locally organised firework displays. Until recently, the tradition was to have a family bonfire, parties and fireworks in the back garden on the night of the 5th itself. The celebration traditionally culminates with the burning of a 'guy' – an effigy of Guy Fawkes – on the bonfire, and here lies the clue to the origins of Bonfire Night.

Guy Fawkes was involved in the infamous gunpowder plot, where Catholic conspirators attempted to blow up the Houses of Parliament at its opening on 5 November 1605. It is this event, or rather its failure, which Bonfire Night commemorates.

Guy's story is not one which ends well, but it is one which begins happily enough – in the city of York.

Guy Fawkes was born in the very centre of York, in a house on Stonegate, among the narrow streets and snickelways which give the city its character. He was baptised just around the corner in the church of St Michael le Belfrey, on 13 April 1570.

Although Guy was born a Protestant, the son of a prominent lawyer in the ecclesiastical courts, his father died when he was eight and his mother remarried a Catholic. Guy moved with them to the village of Scotton

---

TROUBLED TIMES

The gunpowder plot was hatched at a time when English Catholics were bitterly disappointed with James I, the new king. Under Elizabeth I they had been badly persecuted, and hoped James, whose wife was a Catholic, would be more tolerant of their faith. But James was not. It was against this backdrop that the gunpowder plot came about. The long, drawn out and often violent struggle between Catholics and Protestants was set to last for many more years. York was a centre of Catholic resistance throughout the period.

Above *The gunpowder plotters: Thomas Bates, Robert Winter, Christopher Wright, John Wright, Thomas Percy, Guido Fawkes, Robert Catesby, Thomas Winter.*

Right *Guy Fawkes' signature, before and after torture.*

near Knaresborough, and was soon socialising in Catholic circles. He continued his schooling at St Peter's School in York with schoolmates John and Christopher Wright, who would also later participate in the gunpowder plot. It was around this time that the young Guy Fawkes converted to Catholicism.

At the age of twenty-one, Guy sold the land he had inherited in York and joined the Spanish army. He spent the next ten years in Spain, fighting in a religious war against Protestants, and became an expert in explosives. While in Spain, he changed his name to Guido.

It was in London, however, that the gunpowder plot was conceived, at a meeting of five of the plotters in a pub near the Strand. They decided that since Parliament was the place where laws persecuting English Catholics originated, Parliament should be the target. Thomas Percy rented a storeroom under the House of Lords, and over the following months the plotters smuggled in thirty-six barrels of gunpowder. Guy Fawkes' role was to guard the powder, and light it when the time came. If he had succeeded, he would have wiped out the entire royal family, as well as the Lords and the Commons.

However, the plot was inadvertently betrayed by an anonymous letter sent to Lord Mounteagle, urging him not to attend the opening of Parliament as it was to receive a 'terrible blow'. Unfortunately for the plotters, Mounteagle took the letter to Whitehall.

A TRAITOR'S SENTENCE

The barbaric sentence for treason was to be hanged, drawn and quartered. The 'drawing' was the dragging of the prisoner on a wicker hurdle to the place of execution, as he was no longer seen to be fit to tread upon the earth. The rest of the horrific procedure is summed up by Edward Coke, prosecutor at the trial of Guy Fawkes:

> ... he shall be strangled, being hanged up by the neck between heaven and earth as deemed unworthy of both or either ... Then he is to be cut down, and have his privy parts cut off and burnt before his face as being unworthily begotten, and unfit to leave any generation after him. His bowels and inlaid parts taken out and burnt who inwardly had conceived and harboured in his heart such horrible treason. After to have his head cut off, which had imagined the mischief. And lastly, his body to be quartered, and the quarters set up in some high and eminent place to the view and detestation of men, and to become a prey for the fowls of the air.

This grotesque version of the death penalty remained legal in England until 1814.

Guy Fawkes was found and arrested the day before the powder was due to be lit.

Guy was horrifically tortured. At first, when he was caught, he refused to give his true identity or any information about his accomplices. When asked what he was doing with the gunpowder, he told some of the Scots that he intended to have them blown back to their native mountains. He gave his name as John

Storeroom under the House of Lords, where Guy Fawkes was caught with the gunpowder.

Johnson and expressed regret that he had not succeeded in blowing up Parliament. Guy would reveal nothing under questioning, and even the king remarked on his bravery. But this did not stop the king authorising Guy's torture, which he said should be light at first, and increased in severity if necessary.

The two most popular instruments of torture at the time were the manacles and the rack. The manacles were iron gloves, placed on the hands of the victim and by which he was hung from the wall. The procedure would begin with the victim standing on a pile of wood, but this was gradually kicked away until he was left dangling. The pain was excruciating, and the manacles could be tightened to increase the agony. On the rack, the victim's body was gradually stretched, usually dislocating arms and legs, and causing permanent physical damage. We know that the manacles were definitely used on Guy Fawkes, and it is thought that he was also racked.

Prisoner on the rack.

At first Guy managed to remain silent under torture, but on the second day he cracked, and revealed his true identity. On the third day, he revealed the identity of his co-conspirators. Guy Fawkes' signature on his confession after undergoing torture is little more than a scrawl, and reveals the effect the ordeal had had on him.

The plotters' trial was held in Westminster Hall on 27 January 1606. They were all found guilty of treason and sentenced to death by hanging, drawing and quartering. Guy was executed last. He was so broken by the torture that he needed help to mount the scaffold, but mercifully he managed to jump from it and break his neck, dying instantly. His body parts were sent to the four corners of the kingdom as a warning to other would-be plotters.

Although Guy Fawkes was not the main conspirator in the gunpowder plot, he was the one who was caught in the act. The famous image of the man in the storeroom under the Houses of Parliament became imprinted on the public imagination, and Guy Fawkes is the one traditionally remembered on Bonfire Night.

JUNE 1644

THE SIEGE OF YORK

AND A BLOODY SKIRMISH ON THE BOWLING GREEN

In June 1644, for the first time in history, York was surrounded and under siege. The formidable medieval fortress town had been built for an emergency like this. And finally, some 200 years after the end of the medieval period, the time had come. The city walls were about to be put well and truly to the test.

York had been dragged reluctantly into the Civil War, and was divided by the conflict's central issues. But when Charles I took refuge in the city for sixth months, its fate as a Royalist stronghold was sealed. Now, some 4,000 Royalist soldiers under the Marquess of Newcastle were garrisoned behind the city walls. The outlook from the top of those walls, however, must have been extremely bleak. Three hostile

Royalist baggage train arrives at Micklegate Bar.

Parliamentarian armies had the city completely encircled.

The biggest of the enemy armies was that of York's most feared foe, the Scots, under the command of Lord Leven. They numbered 22,000 men, and were positioned on the west bank of the Ouse, in a line extending from Poppleton to Fulford. The Scots had been there since April, and their presence was highly unsettling for the people of York. On the Ouse's east bank, from Fulford to Layerthorpe Bridge, was the Yorkshire Army under Ferdinando, Lord Fairfax, and Sir Thomas Fairfax, who had a further 6,000 men. The final northern section, from Clifton to Layerthorpe, had at first been unoccupied, but now the Army of the Eastern Association, under the Earl of Manchester and Oliver Cromwell, had arrived to fill it, with another 7,000 men. Together, the hostile armies totalled 35,000 men.

The Marquess of Newcastle had written to the king back in April, pleading for a relief force to be sent: '... they have already put themselves in such a posture as will soon ruin us, being at York unless there is some speedy course taken to give us relief, and that with a considerable force, for their army is very strong ... We shall be distressed here very shortly.' But weeks passed and no help from the king arrived.

The garrison had at least been able to strengthen the city defences while it was waiting, and the 3.25 miles of high stone walls encircling York were every bit as formidable as had always been intended. Defensive ditches were on either side, and the four great gates, Micklegate, Bootham, Monkgate and Walmgate, were each protected by a barbican, a

Clifford's Tower, c. 1680.

portcullis and massive doors. Artillery had been mounted on the gateways, on many of the interval towers and other strategic places along the walls. A cannon was mounted on Clifford's Tower, commanding long sections of the walls and fields beyond, and there were guns placed outside the walls, protecting the approaches into the city. But the enemy had also mounted guns, trained right on the city.

With all three armies in place, the besiegers began firing on York. Lord Fairfax had erected a battery of guns on Lamel Hill, some 300 yards from Walmgate Bar. One of the guns carried 'a sixty pound bullet', a formidable weapon by the standards of the time. But the besieged also 'pressed home their attacks fiercely and relentlessly'.

Rather belatedly, the garrison sent out parties to burn the suburbs outside the city walls, so that cover would be denied to would-be snipers or miners. But the besiegers had already started laying mines. One mine, under Walmgate Bar, was quickly discovered, but a second one was not. This undiscovered mine was under St Mary's Tower, just outside Bootham Bar.

The Marquess of Newcastle was desperate to get word to the king, to let him know the situation was

Parliamentarian pikemen (Sealed Knot re-enactors).

St Mary's Tower. Many men were buried in the rubble when it was blown up on 16 June 1644.

now desperate. To play for time, he organised a parley, insisting that hostilities be ceased while it was taking place. Newcastle managed to spin the supposed negotiations out from the 8 to the 15 of June, during which time all was quiet. But the Parliamentarians eventually realised he had no serious intentions of surrendering, and broke off the discussions.

At noon on 16 June, with many of the Royalists still at Matins in the Minster, a detachment of Manchester's men positioned by St Mary's Tower exploded the mine underneath it. Part of the tower was blown up, and as the wall fell outwards, 600 men with ladders, scaling equipment and weapons entered the breach. Others, who failed to get out of the way in time, were crushed by falling rubble. The attackers rushed through the garden, orchard and bowling green, and some even seem to have reached the King's Manor. But a ferocious counterattack from the garrison drove them back. Some Royalists climbed onto the high walls surrounding the bowling green, firing down on the invaders from above. Another Royalist force went out through the breach to defend it from the outside, and seal off a means of retreat. The attack was a complete failure, with over 300 Parliamentarians killed or captured. The Royalists lost just thirty men, including four officers.

The following extract from the diary of Simpon Ashe, chaplain to the Earl of Manchester, describes the scenes which followed:

On Munday morning, some of our souldiers betwixt nine and ten a clock, approaching towards the place where the tower stood, heard in the rubbish a very dolefull cry, some calling, Help, help; others Water, water. Their lamentable complaints moved our men to resolve their relief: so they digged one out dead in the rubbish and brought two alive; but from the Town, such fierce opposition was made by the merciless enemy against our Souldiers while they were labouring to save their friends' lives, that they were compelled to leave many poore distressed ones dying in the dust. Upon Wednesday or Thursday we obtained an hour's time to bury our dead.

For the remainder of the siege, there were no more attempts on the walls. There were also now reports that Prince Rupert of the Rhine, the nephew of the king, was on the way to relieve the York garrison. Prince Rupert had something of a reputation for invincibility, so the Parliamentarian armies were on their guard. In the very early hours of 1 July, hearing that Rupert was approaching, the besieging armies moved off to intercept him. As daylight dawned, the York Garrison found the enemy was gone. The first stage of the siege was abruptly over, but now there was a new battle to fight. Prince Rupert intended to confront the Parliamentarians on Marston Moor. There, the next day, five armies would clash.

THE BATTLE OF MARSTON MOOR

WHERE 'DEAD BODIES LAY THREE MILE IN LENGTH' ALONG THE ROAD TO YORK

The stormy evening of 2 July 1644 saw the biggest and bloodiest battle of the Civil War, as five armies clashed on Marston Moor, just outside York. After only an hour and a half, over 4,000 men were dead or dying on the moor itself, and the road back to York was strewn with the corpses of those who had attempted to flee. Often described as more of a slaughter than a battle, it was also the first occasion in the Civil War where no quarter was shown to the defeated enemy.

Events had begun the day before, when Prince Rupert of the Rhine, nephew of the king, had finally arrived in the vicinity of York. Living up to his reputation of invincibility, Prince Rupert had approached York via an extremely circuitous route, completely evading the enemy who ended up waiting to intercept him in the wrong place. Rupert approached York from the north, sending word to garrison commander, the Marquess of Newcastle, to meet him at dawn on 2 July on Marston Moor. His intention was to engage the Parliamentarians in battle.

Marston Moor was the rendezvous point of the Parliamentarian armies, but only around 3,000 of them were currently there; the others were away waiting in vain for Prince Rupert. By nine o'clock Rupert's men, who had been using the enemy's bridge of boats

Illuftriſſ: & Excellen: Princeps, Rupertus, Comes Palatinus ad Rhœnit., Serenisſ: & Poten: Caroli . Magnæ Britt: &: Regis, Suprem: & Genera: Equitū Dux.

Prince Rupert of the Rhine, who was widely considered invincible until this battle. At Marston Moor, he famously hid from the Parliamentarians in a bean field. (With kind permission of the Thomas Fisher Rare Book Library, University of Toronto)

Marston Moor battlefield.

to cross the river Ouse since dawn, were in place and ready for battle. It was a brilliant manoeuvre. Unfortunately, the Marquess of Newcastle's men were late arriving. The Marquess himself arrived at nine, where Prince Rupert coldly told him, 'My Lord, I wish you had come sooner with your forces.' But more time passed, and there was no sign of the York garrison. They had apparently been looting the vacated Parliamentarian positions outside the city walls, and did not begin to arrive at Marston Moor until two o'clock that afternoon. Prince Rupert must have been furious as he watched the opposition forces building.

The two sides, Parliamentarians and Royalists, faced each other across Tockwith Lane for the entire day, until the Royalists had lost all the advantage of Prince Rupert's surprise arrival. Neither side initiated fighting, however, and by seven in the evening it looked as though there would be none that day. The Royalists began to prepare food, smoke from their campfires sending the signal to the enemy that they were no longer on guard.

At this point, the Parliamentarians decided to charge. According to Simon Ashe, chaplain to the Earl of Manchester,

'Our Army with its several parts moving down the hill was like unto so many thick clouds.' 24,000 Parliamentarians advanced to the beating of drums, their colours flying.

The Royalists had been caught off guard, and the ensuing battle was as chaotic as it was fierce. At one point Sir Thomas Fairfax found himself surrounded by the enemy, but he was not recognised. He took off the white hat band, which identified him as a Parliamentarian, and 'passed through them for one of their own commanders' until he got back to his own men.

Oliver Cromwell led a devastating attack on the Royalist cavalry. He later described it:

> The left wing, which I commanded, being our own horse, saving a few Scots in our rear, beat all the Prince's horse.

Oliver Cromwell, whose successful deployment of his cavalry against the Royalists was a major factor in securing the outcome of the battle.

GHOSTLY PHENOMENA ON BLOODY LANE

There have been numerous reports of paranormal phenomena in the vicinity of Marston Moor, particularly along Tockwith Lane (known locally as Bloody Lane) which runs through the middle of the battlefield. The most common are sightings of weary soldiers in seventeenth-century attire and there is a local legend of a headless horseman. Other people walking in the area have experienced feelings of 'oppression' and of being unable to leave the moor. Battle cries and the sound of soldiers clashing have been reported.

God made them stubble to our swords. We charged their regiments of foot with our horse, and routed all we charged.

The Royalists had been routed. Prince Rupert fled, and famously hid in a bean field till he could get safely back to York. The Marquess of Newcastle's crack regiment, the Whitecoats, refused to flee however. They had fought themselves into a corner, but would accept no quarter and fought on, down to the last man. The Duchess of Newcastle later said that 'they showed such extraordinary valour and courage in that action that they were killed in rank and file.' After the fall of the Whitecoats, it was all over. What was left of the Royalist army either surrendered or attempted to get to back to York. A Parliamentarian soldier describes how they were pursued: 'About nine of the clock we had cleared the field of all enemies ... And followed the chase of them within a mile of Yorke, cutting them down so that their dead bodies lay three miles in length.'

For the remaining hour or so of daylight, and then by moonlight, soldiers stripped and looted the bodies of the dead and dying, taking whatever gold, silver and personal items they could find. When dawn broke the following morning, '...there was a mortifying object to behold, when the naked bodies of thousands lay upon the ground and many not altogether dead' (Simon Ashe). Any soldiers still alive were finished off with knives or poleaxes, and men from local villages were paid to load the bodies into carts and tip them into mass burial pits. The burial pits have never been found.

For those Royalists who managed to make it back to York, there was not necessarily a welcome waiting. Sir Henry Slingsby reported, 'At the Bar none was suffered to come in but such as were of the town, so that the whole street was thronged up to the bar with wounded and lame people, which made a pitiful cry among them.' York's Governor had closed the city gates, to keep out the Parliamentarian cavalry.

After Marston Moor, Royalist activity in the north of England was almost completely over. Little was left of Newcastle's much feared northern army, and Prince Rupert's reputation had been severely shaken. It was the beginning of the end for the Royalists. Two weeks later, on 16 July, the Siege of York finally ended and the city was forced to capitulate. The Parliamentarian Lord Fairfax was named as Governor of the City.

AD 1739

DICK TURPIN

THE KNAVESMIRE VILLAIN WHO BECAME A LEGEND

The Dick Turpin known by most people is the heroic highwayman in the tricorn hat. He carries two pistols, wears a frock coat and riding boots, and famously rides his horse Black Bess in an epic run from London to York. He is a courageous, admirable figure, not unlike Robin Hood, robbing from the rich to give to the poor. But this Dick Turpin is a mythical one, created during the Victorian period by the writer William Harrison Ainsworth. The story of the man himself is much less romantic.

In October 1738, a man known as John Palmer was apprehended and put in York Castle Prison. He was an unpleasant character, of average height and with a pockmarked face. He was arrested for shooting a cockerel. After a disappointing day's hunting, Palmer had lost his temper and he shot the cockerel on his return to Brough, where he lodged at the Ferryman Inn. When challenged, Palmer threatened to shoot the complainant too.

As the police made enquiries about John Palmer, they found that he was wanted in Lincolnshire for horse theft,

as well as various other crimes. But an even bigger surprise was to come. Palmer had written a letter to his brother-in-law in Essex, asking for help. When the letter fell into the hands of the police, Palmer was found to be none other than the notorious highway robber Dick Turpin.

The real Dick Turpin was a callous thug, who had committed a series of violent armed robberies and murdered the servant of a keeper in Epping Forest. He had been England's most wanted criminal for quite some time, with a £200 bounty on his head. The real Turpin was no hero, and if he was famous in his time it was only for the horror and cruelty of his offences. Originally from Essex, Dick Turpin had joined a local gang involved in poaching, but their crimes had rapidly escalated. On the run in Yorkshire, he had taken on the new identity of John Palmer, but after the incident with the cockerel his game was up.

At York's Winter Assizes on 22 March 1739, Dick Turpin was found guilty on two counts of horse theft, and the death sentence was passed.

Defiant to the last, Turpin appeared unconcerned about his fate, and seems to have decided to go out in style. The day before his execution, a new frock coat and pumps were delivered to him in his cell, and he had hired four men to act as his mourners and make sure he was given a decent burial. He gave out hatbands and gloves, and to a married woman with whom he'd been having an affair, a gold ring and two pairs of shoes.

On Saturday, 7 April 1739, Turpin was taken in a cart from York Castle Prison, through the town, and out of Micklegate Bar to the Knavesmire. He was accompanied by another man, John Stead, also convicted of horse stealing. The Sheriff of Yorkshire had provided a strong guard on the day, expecting an attempted escape, but none was made. Turpin had apparently accepted his fate. As he approached the gallows, he 'behav'd himself with amazing assurance' and 'bow'd to the spectators as he passed.' It was only as he mounted the ladder to the gallows that there was a slight trembling in his left leg, 'which he stamped down with an air' then looked around at the crowd 'with undaunted courage'. After a few words, Turpin jumped from the ladder and died immediately. His body was left hanging on the Knavesmire till three o'clock in the afternoon, when it was cut down and laid out in the Blue Boar Tavern in Castlegate.

On Sunday 8 April, Turpin was buried in St George's churchyard at Fishergate. The men he had employed as mourners did a good job, burying him deeply and well. Since it was customary for the bodies of executed criminals to be given up for medical dissection, particular care had to be taken. But in the early hours of Tuesday morning, Turpin's body was dug up and stolen. The phenomenon of

Dick Turpin hiding in a cave in Epping Forest.

body snatching was very unpopular, and it was not long before an angry mob of locals had stolen it back. They brought it 'through the streets of the city, in a sort of triumph, almost naked, being only laid on a board cover'd with some straw and carried on four men's shoulders ...' It was then buried back in the same grave, covered with lime to make it useless for dissection.

And that would have been the end of Dick Turpin, had it not been for a certain Victorian writer. William Harrison Ainsworth's novel *Rookwood* was published in 1834. It was hugely successful, and made Ainsworth into one of the most popular writers of the era. The novel featured a dashing highwayman, Dick Turpin, and though the character was based on the real man, he was romanticised beyond all recognition:

> Rash daring was the main feature of Turpin's character. Like our great Nelson, he knew fear only by name ... possessed of the belief that his hour was not yet come, he cared little or nothing for any risk he might incur ... With him expired the chivalrous spirit which animated so many knights of the road; with him died away that passionate love of enterprise, that high spirit of devotion to the fair sex...

The novel was a good and exciting read, fixing the mythical Dick Turpin into the minds of generations to come, along with his fictional horse Black Bess in their legendary ride up the Great North Road: 'Now they are buried in the darkness of woods; now sweeping along on the wide plain; now clearing the unopened toll-bar; now trampling over the hollow-sounding bridge, their shadows momentarily reflected in the placid mirror of the stream.' Black Bess, who died from exhaustion on arrival at York, became just as famous as Turpin himself.

A grave which is supposedly that of Dick Turpin can still be seen in St George's churchyard in Fishergate. It is worth pointing out, however, that the headstone dates from later than 1739, and also seems to be later than the headstones in the churchyard. It is also unusually large, perhaps to tie in with the local legend that Turpin is not buried alone in there – he is accompanied by Black Bess!

Dick Turpin's gravestone at St George's churchyard in York.

AD 1829

THE YORK MINSTER ARSONIST

York Minster is one of the most magnificent medieval buildings in the country. Its origins are rooted in the earliest history of both York and of England, and it has always been revered by the citizens of York as a treasure in their midst. Yet in 1829, one York resident believed it was his divine mission to burn the Minster down.

Jonathan Martin had issued five warnings, but no-one paid them any attention. Pinned to the Minster door, fastened to the choir gates or wrapped around a brick and left in the nave, his scrawled, badly spelled messages told of forthcoming judgement on the clergy: 'Your gret Charichis and Minstairs will cume rattling down upon your gilty heads.' But the Minster clergy were quite used to religious eccentrics with grievances, and although the letters were odd, the threats they contained were not taken seriously. Jonathan Martin however, meant every word he wrote.

Martin hugely disapproved of the way the Minster was run. He felt it was operating as an elitist venue for York's high society rather than a place of worship, where all were equal in the sight of God. The dean and canon were indeed very much part of York's social scene, and attended engagements such as dinners, parties, balls and concerts. In the Minster itself, secular musical concerts were held and the nave was used as place where the well-to-do would go for their Sunday afternoon

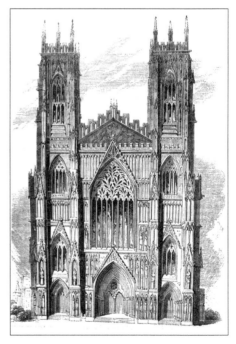

York Minster's West Front.

stroll. There were many at the time who would have agreed with Martin on these issues.

But for Jonathan Martin, it did not stop there. He believed that God wanted to punish the Church for acting in this way. He also thought that it was his duty to give out the warnings, and to exact the punishment if the clergy did not change their ways. After a dream, in which an immense black cloud moved from above his own place of residence and settled over the Minster, Martin became convinced God wanted him to burn down the great cathedral church as retribution.

On the evening of 1 February 1829, Martin attended Evensong and stayed behind after the service, hiding behind a monument until everyone had left. Once the doors were locked, he crept out into the darkness and set about his task.

A boy who arrived early for morning choir practice the next day was the first to notice the smoke. The choir, where the services were performed, was on fire. A crowd gathered, and an emergency fire team was called to the scene, but it was poorly equipped to deal with an emergency of this magnitude. Flames had completely engulfed the choir.

York Minster Choir.

The fire raged, and as it did so, a bizarre phenomenon occurred: the organ began to play on its own. It was a groaning, discordant noise, which must have sounded quite terrifying to those on the scene. The hot air from the fire was being sucked up through the pipes of the organ, causing it to play. But worse was to come; the organ was

---

A DISCOVERY UNDER THE MINSTER FLOOR

While clearing up after the fire, antiquarian John Brown and a team of workmen found the top of a column under the floor of the choir. Amazed, they dug down to see what else might be there. They discovered the skeleton of a building which was very different from the current Minster. What they had found was the remains of the first Norman church on the site, constructed by Thomas of Bayeux in 1080. Its remains can be seen today in the Minster Undercroft.

FURTHER FIRES AT THE MINSTER

There have been two other major fires in York Minster since 1829. The first was in 1840 when workmen left a candle burning in the south-west tower and the nave roof was once again seriously damaged. The second was in 1984, and it caused extensive damage to the roof of the south transept and the Rose Window. This more recent fire was most probably caused by lightning.

acting like a chimney and conducted the fire upwards to the roof. Soon the fourteenth-century vaulted oak ceiling was ablaze, with streams of molten lead pouring down into the choir below. At nine o'clock the roof collapsed, causing an almost apocalyptic scene, the air so thick with dust that daylight turned to darkness. The fall of the roof helped to smother the flames and, eventually, the fire started to die down, but the choir was left in ruins. The beautiful vaulted ceiling, the choir stalls, the pulpit, the archbishop's throne and the organ were all gone. Even pillars of magnesian limestone had melted away.

The people of York were outraged that the Minster, which had dominated York's skyline since further back than anyone could remember, had been deliberately set alight. Jonathan Martin's warning notes, on which he had signed his name, were at this point remembered. A great manhunt was launched, and the culprit was arrested.

Jonathan Martin's trial on 26 March was a huge event. He had aroused the curiosity of everyone in town. Tickets had to be issued in advance as there were worries the number of people at court would be too great. The newspapers reported on those attending and their attire, as though it were a society event. They also reported that Martin did not look at all concerned, frequently smiling at the onlookers.

There was never any question as to whether or not Martin had deliberately set fire to the Minster, as he did not deny it and was even proud of what he had done, believing that he had obeyed the voice of God. What needed to be determined by the jury was whether or not he was of sound mind. If he was not, then he would escape the hanging which would otherwise be the obligatory sentence. Some friends and acquaintances, not realising they were actually doing him no favours, testified that he seemed perfectly normal. But doctors who had visited him in prison declared that Martin suffered from monomania, a condition where insanity is confined to one area only, in this case religion.

The jury reached its verdict in seven minutes. Martin was found to be not guilty on the grounds of insanity. He had escaped the death penalty, but was committed to the lunatic asylum Bedlam for the rest of his life. Here, he spent the rest of his days producing apocalyptic drawings of God burning down cathedrals. He died in Bedlam in 1838.

AD 1832

CHOLERA EPIDEMIC

DEATH AMID FILTH AND SQUALOR

Modern-day visitors arriving in York by train may choose to take the short walk from the station into town. In doing so they will pass by a small rectangular patch of land, where Victorian gravestones lurch at angles among topiaried yews. It would be easy to hurry by and overlook just one more piece of the past in a history-packed city. But the Cholera Burial Ground is a place with a story to tell, for those who have time to seek it out.

The burial ground dates from a time when visitors arriving in York came not by train, but by stagecoach or boat. On 28 May 1832, many such visitors were arriving for the races. They included a party of vagrants who came in by ferry on the polluted river Ouse, with ferryman Thomas Hughes. Hughes lived in Beedham's Court off Skeldergate, a filthy and overcrowded slum known locally as the Hagworm's Nest. Along with the party, there travelled also a killer, one which the people of York had been expecting, but for which they were still tragically unprepared. The killer was

Memorial stone in the Cholera Burial Ground.

The Water Lanes, c. 1813.

cholera, a disease that infected the lower intestine, causing profuse diarrhoea and vomiting, usually resulting in death.

Within a week, local papers were reporting on an outbreak of cholera and its first victims:

> The disease has at last manifested itself in our city. The first alarm was on Sunday when a poor man named Hughes residing in The Hagworm's Nest became ill ... The next was Greaves, a sawyer living in the same court. He went home intoxicated on Monday night and was a corpse on Tuesday night. Barrett who kept The Anchor in Middle Water Lane became ill on Tuesday and died the next day ...

Hughes infected his own family, other residents of the Hagworm's Nest and Mr Barrett, the publican of the Anchor Inn in Middle Water Lane, which he

had visited just before his symptoms appeared. The whole Barrett family became ill and were loaned a commode chair by a friend in the Shambles. It was returned in such a foul state that a neighbour, not having managed to clean it, threw it into the river Ouse. Within a week, cholera was on the rampage in York. In the second week, almost every house in the Water Lanes, another slum area, had a case of cholera.

No-one knew what caused cholera, or how to prevent and treat it. A prevalent idea was the miasma theory – that illness is caused by foul air. It was thought that if the cause of the smell was eradicated, then the illness would also be eliminated. There had already been a mass clean-up in York as a preventative measure, and now there was a renewed cleaning frenzy. Streets were washed with quicklime and fumigated with burning tar. Houses were whitewashed, and the stagnant city moats were emptied by night and disinfected.

No attention was paid to the river Ouse. As usual, the city's sewage was discharged into it and, as usual, people fetched their drinking water supplies from it. The deaths continued.

Medical treatment for cholera was at an experimental stage. Rectal injections of turpentine and oral doses of calomel, a mercury compound, were among the catalogue of horrors administered to patients. Tragically, a complete abstinence from all fluids was also usually recommended. Rehydration is in fact key to the successful treatment of the infection. The local paper, *The Gazette*, blamed cholera on 'the poor and depraved' and cited its causes as a

QUACK REMEDIES

Morison's Pills, which purged the stomach through 'easy upward and downward evacuations' was one of the many quack treatments York people tried to ward off cholera. Mrs Anne Swaine of Walmgate, writing to the local paper in 1832, was obviously impressed:

> The violent pains in my side could not be cured by the York dispensary, or by any medical man in this city, but fifteen Morison's Pills per night for three weeks caused me to quit such a quantity of bile and corruption from my stomach and bowels that I was a wonder to all who witnessed it. I have now discharged my maid, do all my own housework and can walk ten miles a day.

Another quack remedy was Bile Beans. These were popular in the Victorian era, and the first half of the twentieth century. They contained a laxative, but also claimed to treat piles, female weakness, sallow complexions, pimples, impure blood and bowel troubles.

A Bile Beans advertisement,
Lord Mayor's Walk.

lack of cleanliness, intemperance and low-living.

The epidemic peaked in the first week of July, with 128 cases and 40 deaths. It then gradually began to wane and finally, on 15 October, the *Herald* reported that it was finished. There had been a total of 450 cholera cases, with 185 deaths, among a population of 25,357.

In the aftermath of the epidemic, it was discovered that there were no drains in the streets where the infection rate was at its highest. In a report commissioned in 1844, it was noted that the cholera epidemic in York seemed fatal to the people in proportion to the deficience of drainage in their locality. There was a further major cholera epidemic in York in 1849. It was not until 1854, however, that the York-born physician John Snow discovered that cholera was caused by contaminated water rather than by bad smells, and the way to prevent it was to ensure sewage and drinking water were properly separated. It was to take almost another decade for his ideas to become widely accepted.

GEORGE GODDARD

AN ANCESTOR IN YORK CASTLE PRISON

While researching my own family history, in a project quite separate from the writing of this book, it was brought home to me just how much of a dark shadow York Castle Prison could cast over the lives of ordinary Yorkshire folk, for in late middle-age, my five times great-grandfather George Goddard was uprooted from the West Yorkshire village of Holmfirth, where he had lived all his life, and was incarcerated in York Castle Prison. George was a weaver, and a family man who lived in a close-knit community with his children and other relatives all nearby. What had he done to suddenly merit imprisonment in the distant capital of the county, and the title of 'convicted felon'?

As I went through the criminal registers, newspaper reports of the time and the York Castle gaoler's journal, a different story of George's life began to emerge. My ancestor, it seemed, had likely been leading a double life. He was gay, in a time when homosexuality was not tolerated and the language used to describe it was redolent with Old Testament condemnation.

In the *Morning Post* of 23 December 1850, it was reported that George Goddard had been tried along with one Thomas Whittaker for 'an abominable offence with each other'. In his summing-up speech, Mr Justice Patterson said: 'It is a horrible and most detestable offence, alike in the sight of God and man – an offence for which the Almighty has, in years past, destroyed a whole district by fire and brimstone from heaven. My duty is to pass upon you the sentence of the law. It is impossible for me to do otherwise than to pass that sentence.'

The sentence was death by hanging, and that it had been passed was recorded in the journal of Mr Noble, gaoler at York Castle Prison. Mr Noble very rarely mentioned prisoners by name, or details of their cases, but seems to have taken an interest in the case of my ancestor. He mentions that George was taken very ill just before his trial, so much so that Mr Noble felt moved to send for family members from Holmfirth to visit him. A few days later he mentions that George was much better, having received a visit from his son-in-law. From the gaoler's concern, and a very long summing-up speech from the judge, Justice Patterson, who repeatedly stated that this was not his sentence but the

YORK CASTLE PRISON

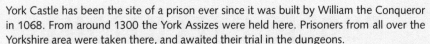

York Castle has been the site of a prison ever since it was built by William the Conqueror in 1068. From around 1300 the York Assizes were held here. Prisoners from all over the Yorkshire area were taken there, and awaited their trial in the dungeons.

Between 1700 and 1705 the old prison buildings were demolished and a new country jail was built. This is now part of the York Castle Museum, and actual cells where eighteenth-century prisoners were incarcerated, including Dick Turpin, can be visited there.

Criminal business must have been booming, because in 1835 a third, much larger prison was built right next to Clifford's Tower. It was to this building that my own ancestor George Goddard would have been brought in 1850. York Castle dominated the Yorkshire criminal justice process right through until 1864, when cases from West Yorkshire were moved to Leeds for trial.

In 1900, York Castle became a military prison, but did not survive for long afterwards. In 1929 the whole complex was bought by the local authorities, and the Victorian prison was immediately demolished, with no trace of it remaining today. In 1938, York Castle Museum opened in the eighteenth-century building.

York Crown Court is still held in the eighteenth-century courthouse. It has holding cells and dispenses justice to those accused of serious crimes, as it has done for the last 1,000 years.

The 'Eye of York'. The seventeenth-century prison in the middle of this picture now houses part of the Castle Museum. The now demolished nineteenth-century prison would have stood in the foreground here, just in front of Clifford's Tower, from which this view was taken.

law's, you get the impression that those in authority were struggling to find the death penalty appropriate.

On Christmas Day 1850, Mr Noble made a final entry in his journal regarding my ancestor and Thomas Whittaker: he had received a sentence reprieve for them and had just been to remove them from the condemned cell. One can only imagine the relief the two men must have felt. Their new sentence, however, was one which was probably almost as terrifying: transportation to the colony of Australia for life.

I have as yet been unable to find any further records for George Goddard, either of his death or his transportation, but know that he was still in York Gaol on 30 March 1851, the night of the census. It is certain that he will never have been allowed to return to Holmfirth. Ten years later, in 1861, England's sodomy laws were reformed and the death sentence could no longer be applied.

PUBLIC EXECUTIONS AT YORK

AN ENTERTAINING DAY OUT

Throughout much of history, York has been a city of gallows. For as long as justice has been dispensed from the capital of the north, executions have been taking place here too, heads frequently adorning the walls and bars. Executions have taken place more or less all over the city – although nowhere so many as on the Knavesmire – and going to watch them was seen as great entertainment.

The tradition of public executions goes back a long way. Some of the very first gallows in York were established in accordance with the Anglo-Saxon concept of Ingangtheof, where a landowner had the right to execute criminals caught within the borders of his own land. Many gallows remained for centuries after the Anglo-Saxon period, including those at Foss Bridge and at the Horse Fair. Religious institutions also had their own courts and could dish out the death penalty. In around 1135, Holy Trinity Priory was given the right to set up gallows, which were probably situated near the Knavesmire Gates. These were known as the Thieves' Gallows.

Then on 7 March 1379, the City Gallows were set up on the Knavesmire.

They were at the city boundary on the road to London; these gallows became known as York Tyburn, after the ones in London, and would be York's main place of execution for the next 400 years. The gallows itself was a distinctive wooden construction, with a triangular frame set high on three wooden legs. It was known locally as the 'three-legged mare' and also 'the Tyburn tree'.

The transporting of criminals to the Knavesmire was a familiar ritual. The prisoner was taken from York Castle Prison by sledge or hurdle, and later by cart, first along Castlegate and then up Micklegate, and out of the city walls via Micklegate Bar. Crowds of people would accompany them along the way, either jeering and shouting or offering encouragement, depending on who the criminal was. On the Knavesmire, thousands of people would be waiting to watch the proceedings, some of whom had been there all night for a place at the front.

Execution memorabilia such as chapbooks (souvenir pocket booklets) ballads and copies of last speeches were sold, and ale and pie sellers brought refreshments to the crowds. Other forms of entertainment were also

Medieval prisoners being taken to their execution.

put on, and here the York Races had its beginnings, among the sideshows to the executions. Some of the first bookmakers on the Knavesmire took bets on how long it would take people to die on the gallows.

The first man hanged on the Knavesmire was Private Edward Hewison, aged twenty, a soldier serving with the Earl of Northumberland's Light Horse. He had raped a servant girl from Sheriff Hutton Castle as she was making her way into York. Hewison was apprehended the next day, and executed on 31 March 1379. After execution his body was hung in a gibbet near the scene of the crime. Strangely, the last man to be hanged on the Knavesmire 400 years later had a very similar name to the first, and was also a soldier who had committed rape. Private Edward Hughes, nineteen, of the 18th Light Dragoons, was executed on 29 August 1801.

Over the years in between, hundreds were executed at the Knavesmire gallows. It was not only hangings which took place here, but beheadings too. This punishment was often meted out to nobles, as it was seen as less degrading than hanging, and usually killed them more quickly. Murder, burglary, highway robbery, coining (counterfeiting money), arson and theft were all crimes which could incur the death penalty. For those who committed high treason, the grisly traitor's fate of being hanged, drawn and quartered was reserved, and this too took place on the Knavesmire.

'High treason' was often a case of practising the wrong religion at the wrong time, and many of those executed in this barbaric way were religious martyrs. On Good Friday 1570, four of the Catholics who had taken part in the Northern Rebellion of 1569 were hanged, drawn and quartered on the Knavesmire. One of the two leaders of the Rebellion, the Earl of Northumberland, was beheaded two years later, in the marketplace at Pavement (see panel).

Surprisingly, it was as late as the eighteenth century that the last hangings, drawings and quarterings took place in York. In November 1746, twenty-three rebels who had taken part in the Jacobite Rebellion suffered the barbaric fate on the Knavesmire. Two of them, William Connolly and

THE EXECUTION OF
THE EARL OF NORTHUMBERLAND, 1572

Thomas Percy, the 7th Earl of Northumberland, was one of the leaders of the Northern Rebellion against Queen Elizabeth I. It was a Catholic rebellion, seeking to replace Elizabeth with Mary, Queen of Scots. Percy had sought refuge in Scotland, but was purchased from the Scots for £2,000 so that he could be executed in York, a Catholic stronghold. But the plan to terrify the people into submission through his public execution backfired spectacularly.

Thomas Percy was a man of strong character, and an excellent orator. In his last address, he had the crowd's rapt attention as he proclaimed his faith as the source of his strength. He declared that if he had a thousand lives, he would give them all up for the Catholic faith. 'As for this new English Church,' he said, 'I do not acknowledge it.'

Percy was beheaded in the marketplace, in front of All Saints' church. He faced his death with dignity and courage. After asking the forgiveness of the crowd, he declared he forgave all from the bottom of his heart, and placed his head on the scaffold. As soon as the executioner's axe had descended, the scaffold was swarming with people, collecting his blood on handkerchiefs and clothes as relics of a martyr.

Replica gloves, sword and helmet of the Earl of Northumberland, in All Saints' church, Pavement.

Former site of the gallows on the Knavesmire.

James Mayne, were the last to have their heads impaled on the Micklegate Bar. Their heads were stolen by Jacobite sympathisers in 1754.

After 1801, executions were moved to York Castle Prison itself so that 'the entrance to the town should no longer be annoyed by dragging criminals through the streets'. Travellers arriving from the south had objected to the spectacle as they arrived in York. The crowds now had to gather on St George's Field opposite the prison for their entertainment on execution day. In 1868 public execution was abolished. From this date, hangings took place inside the prison.

THE REAL SHAMBLES

STREET OF BUTCHERS AND SLAUGHTERHOUSES

York's Shambles, voted Britain's most picturesque street, is visited by thousands every year. Its timber-framed houses, dating from the fourteenth and fifteenth centuries, lean over the cobbles towards one another, making it possible in some places to hold hands across the street. Everyone seems to agree that walking down Shambles is 'like going back in time'. But is it really?

Arrive in Shambles in the 1940s or '50s, and you would find some properties in a sorry state of repair, with no gift shops in sight. Look out for delivery vans – one backed right into one of the buildings around this time, and reduced it to a heap of rubble. Visitors sometimes thought the street was a slum, and regularly asked if it had been condemned.

Go back further to the late 1800s, and you'd see mostly butchers' shops as you walked along, with great hunks of fresh meat hanging from hooks outside the windows. Rather ugly Victorian façades obscured some of the quaint medieval frontages you can see today. You might also notice a definite look of poverty to some of the street's residents.

Travel back further still, to medieval times, and you wouldn't want to arrive on the wrong day of the week, or you could find yourself ankle deep in waste meat, blood and guts. Shambles was the butchers' street, and is thought to have been such since before the Domesday Book of 1085, in which it gets a mention. Twice a week, waste

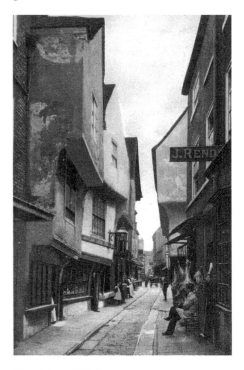

Shambles, c. 1890

IT'S ALL IN THE NAME

Shambles takes its name from the stalls or tables on which meat was displayed, which were known as 'shamels'. As time went on, these stalls became permanent shops, and some of the shamels themselves are visible today, incorporated in the current shops as window ledges. Meat hooks in the windows of some shops can also still be seen.

Shambles was once known as the Great Flesshamels, to distinguish it from the fish shambles on Foss Bridge. It has also sometimes been known as Haymongergate, because the butchers kept animal fodder for the beasts waiting to be slaughtered. Another name used was Needlergate; the making of needles from animal bones was another occupation once practised on the site.

Meat hooks on a Shambles' shop front, clearly visible on the left of the image.

was washed away down the road. Even on an ordinary day, the scene there would have been busy, messy and quite chaotic. Animals were slaughtered on site, with dogs running around, fighting over waste scraps on the bloody cobbles. Tradesmen would have been loudly advertising their wares to passers-by, set out on stalls in the street. You could probably say that the whole place was ... a bit of a shambles.

The way the buildings of Shambles leant over the street, as they still do today, was by design, and had the very functional purpose of providing shade for the meat. But in an age without refrigeration, you can still be sure that the whole street, to put it bluntly, would have stunk. In 1402, complaints

were made by Churchgoers at nearby St John in the Marsh, who said that the Shambles' butchers were using the area around their church as a refuse dump. The stench was such that they could barely manage to sit through services.

The medieval butchers of York were a very prosperous community, and many of the buildings in Shambles date from York's halcyon days in the fourteenth and fifteenth century. It is because of relative poverty after this period that Shambles has altered very little. But it is no surprise that by the twentieth century, decay had set in. It is at this point in history that the Shambles of old became the Shambles that we know today.

During the war years, the dereliction of such ancient buildings did not

A ROYAL DECREE: YORK STINKETH!

— ∞∞ —

In 1332, the mayor and bailiffs of York received the following message on behalf of Edward III. 'The King detesting the abominable smell abounding in the said city more than any other in the realm from dung and manure and other filth and dirt wherewith the streets and lanes are filled and obstructed ... orders them to cause all streets and lanes of the city to be cleansed.'

— ∞∞ —

escape public notice, and led to a report recommending a plan for the street's preservation. The plan was drawn up by the Royal Society for the Preservation of Ancient Buildings and Monuments, which described Shambles as 'a unique example of a medieval street.' At the same time, York Corporation bought up many of the properties, and arranged to have them carefully restored. They were then let out at low rates, to artisans and craftspeople wherever possible, and the image of a thriving medieval street was soon created. In

1970, *The Dalesman* reported that Shambles had been 'literally snatched from death' and that 'the semi-decrepit image has been virtually banished'. It also noted that only three butcher's shops were left in the street. *York and Country Magazine* at around the same time commented, 'It's the shops, their wares, and the craftsmen seen here and there at their jobs that link the past with the present and enchant the modern sightseer.' Today, Shambles is one of the best preserved medieval streets in Europe.

YORK'S SMELLIEST STREET

— ∞∞ —

The Shambles may have run with blood and guts twice a week, and had a dire waste disposal problem, but it was not the smelliest street in town. That accolade goes to Tanner Row, on the opposite side of the river from the city centre. It was located here because the tanners who once practised their trade there had to be confined to the outskirts of town; the process of tanning raw hide into workable leather involved urine, animal faeces and decaying flesh. Today Tanner Row still retains its name – but thankfully not the smell.

— ∞∞ —

ZEPPELINS OVER YORK

GERMAN AIRSHIPS BRING TERROR TO THE SKIES

On 4 August 1914, Britain declared war on Germany. Men were soon signing up in their hundreds to fight in a conflict that everyone thought would be over by Christmas, but the First World War would turn out to be four and half long years of misery. The 200 men enlisting daily in York can have had no idea of the heart-breaking reality of trench warfare which lay ahead for most of them. And in the city of York itself, there was terror on the horizon.

In 1916, halfway through the conflict, there was a series of Zeppelin attacks on York. Zeppelins were a type of huge, rigid aircraft, pioneered in Germany in the late nineteenth century. They had been in use as passenger aircraft since 1910, but the Germans soon put them to use in both reconnaissance and bombing missions. Although Zeppelins soon proved ineffective on bombing raids, they had a strong psychological impact, and caused fear all over Britain.

On the evening of 2 May 1916, the menacing form of one of the dreaded, cigar-shaped airships was spotted over York. The *Herald* reported that

'it remained stationary, with engines turned off, for fully three minutes. Not a bomb was dropped during this time, and it appeared to the onlookers as if the pilot was taking his bearings. When the engines were re-started, the airship with its droning, humming accompaniment of sound, passed over the town. Great volumes of dense black smoke issued from the machine ... floating with marked contrast against the clear and star-bedecked sky.'

The Vow of Vengeance! (Library of Congress, LC-USZC4-11188)

YORK IN THE FIRST WORLD WAR

As a garrison town, York had an important part to play in the war. The City Art Gallery was requisitioned as a recruitment headquarters and schools were taken over to house military personnel. A tented village for soldiers was also set up on the Knavesmire. York also became a detention centre for German civilian prisoners. Conspiracy theories abounded, and German nationals from all over the county were sent to York Castle Prison. A tented overflow camp was even set up on Castle Green, in the centre of the prison complex, and a concentration camp with a capacity for 1,700, surrounded by barbed wire, was set up on Leeman Road. With its large Quaker population, York had many conscientious objectors among its young men called up for service. They had to put their case for a non-combatant role in the war before a tribunal in the Guildhall. Social pressure to fight was such that those who decided to stand up for their beliefs required great courage.

War memorial in the Dean's Park, next to York Minster.

Then the Zeppelin began to discharge its cargo of explosives, and over the next ten minutes eighteen bombs were dropped, taking nine lives and causing forty injuries. On Nunthorpe Avenue, twenty-eight-year-old Emily Chapman was outside, looking at the Zeppelin. She was hit by shrapnel and was killed instantly, while her sister was injured in the spine, and her mother's arm was blown off. In Upper Price Street, a bomb caused a house 'to fall like a pack of cards', killing its occupants: a railway pensioner and his wife, George and Sarah-Ann Avison. It was in the Peasholme Green area, however, that the airship did the most damage. Here, six people were killed, including serviceman Edward Beckett, who was home on a month's leave and had been staying with his mother in Hungate.

Writing about the attack, a local reporter quotes a lady as exclaiming, 'It's a rotten shame!' He then replies, 'It was a rotten shame, madame,' and further comments, 'It was the work of cads.'

A second Zeppelin raid took place in York on the night of 25 September 1916. This time, however, the city was prepared, as 'a powerful anti-aircraft gun and searchlight of great strength' had been installed on the hill near Poppleton Road School. The airship was immediately picked out by the searchlight, and had to manoeuvre itself to safety, dropping its bombs to the east of the city centre. There were no casualties, although six horses were killed and one woman later died of shock. But the attack was widely regarded as a fiasco.

The third and final Zeppelin raid took place on the night of 27 November 1916, and was a spectacular failure. Two Zeppelins came this time, but were swiftly illuminated by the searchlight, and peppered with bullets by the guns. Both had to make a swift retreat, dropping bombs as they did so, but only one person was injured. The atmosphere in York was one of triumph. It seems from a report in the press that people had ignored the police instructions to stay indoors, and that many had been out on the streets, watching the drama unfold:

'Go on! Go on!' were the full-throated cries by hundreds of the inhabitants of a town in the North-Eastern Counties as they witnessed on Monday night a thrilling and exhilarating spectacle of the skies ... Men's nerves tingled with the joy of battle as they saw a hostile invader held for four full minutes in the star-bedecked heavens by a powerful searchlight while the guns belched forth their message ... and at last the climax came when a mighty cheer rent the air, followed by shouts of, 'She's hit!' It was a sound that was good to hear.

The Zeppelins had been seen off, but there were still two years of sadness, hardship and loss to go before the bells of the Minster would finally ring out the end of the First World War. The defeat of the Zeppelins over York that night was a great morale boost, however, and gave York's people a glimmer of hope for the future.

THE KING'S BOOK OF YORK HEROES

In the north transept of York Minster is an extraordinary book of remembrance to the servicemen and women of York who were killed the First World War. The *King's Book of York Heroes* contains the names and photographs of the 1,443 people who were born in York, or resident within its boundaries, and who lost their lives in the service of the crown.

With its elaborately carved oak cover, and metalwork including hinges, padlocks and clasps in oxidised silver, the book is a testament to the amazing skill of York's craftsmen of the time. It was received at York Minster by the Duke of York on 9 November 1920, and was then handed over into the custody of the Dean and Chapter. It is signed on one of the preliminary pages by King George V, who was very impressed with both the concept and the workmanship, taking time to look at each page and asking many questions about the people the book commemorates.

THE BAEDECKER BLITZ

THE NIGHT YORK BURNED

In the early hours of 29 April 1942, the Royal Observer Corps spotted forty German aircraft off the north-east Coast of England. Suddenly, the planes swooped inland to the west, one group over Flamborough Head, the other over Hornsea. It became immediately apparent that they were heading for York.

By 2.30 a.m. they had arrived over the city, and York's worst night of the Second World War had begun. The planes came singularly or in pairs at first, dropping sticks of flares and incendiary bombs over the west of the city. They fell on Pickering Terrace, Bootham Terrace and Burton Stone Lane. People were woken from their sleep to see a strange and unnatural light outside; their streets were burning. It was only after the first incendiaries had fallen that the air raid sirens began to sound. York's residents rallied, ushering people to shelters. There was no time to lose. It was well known that incendiaries were usually a prelude to explosives.

It was not long before high explosives did begin to fall. In Bootham Crescent a fire-fighting team was struggling to

put out the flames. When the first bomb struck, fireman Arthur Broadhead had just gone to see if the hose was properly attached to the hydrant. His co-worker reported that he was blown to bits, and could only be later identified from his signet ring. Arthur's would be the first death of many.

The bombers rapidly turned their attention to York railway station. Passengers arriving in on the 10.15 express from London were greeted by air-raid sirens and a panicked platform announcer telling them to take cover as quickly as they could. Not everyone left the train, however, expecting the alert not to prove serious, and to continue on to Edinburgh. Several minutes later, a 250 pound bomb crashed down, shattering the station's glass roof. At this point, everyone ran for cover. More bombs and incendiaries followed, and soon the entire station was ablaze, including the track and the train itself.

Station staff diligently carried out their duties, attempting to extinguish what they could of the raging flames, but it was an impossible task. Station foreman William Milner ran back into a burning station building to fetch an urgently needed medical kit. He did not re-emerge. Later, when his body was found, he was still holding the box of medical supplies. Today, there is a memorial to him at the station on platform three.

The station was a main target in the raid, and the streets around it were badly hit. The Bar Convent School, just 100 yards away, suffered a direct hit. Three nuns were killed as they rushed to the aid of an elderly sister who had been unable to get down into the cellar, where everyone else was taking shelter. A further two were trapped under debris from the blast.

The German pilots were repeatedly swooping down over York, riddling streets with machine-gun fire and dropping more explosives and incendiaries. Coney Street was attacked by fire bombs, and the offices of *The Press* were soon burning, as was a Rowntree's warehouse by the Ouse, filled with bags of sugar.

By 3 a.m. flames had taken hold in the city's medieval Guildhall and the ancient church of St Martin-le-grand. Both buildings were eventually gutted by fire. Nearby, thanks to the hard work of those on duty, the eighteenth-century Assembly Rooms and the Mansion House were saved.

Meanwhile, the casualty figures were mounting. At Kent Street, the city's emergency mortuary was in operation, and the scene there was distressing. It was rapidly filling with bodies, many of them in a mangled mess, and covered with pieces of rubble and brick. One or two consisted of just a few remains in a bucket. A deceased young mother lay on a metal stretcher, her child dead in her arms.

Arthur Broadhead's headstone in York Cemetery reads, 'Killed in action in Bootham Crescent.'

Frantic work went on through the night to free those trapped in the wreckage of bombed houses. Sometimes they would be brought out alive; other times not. Although the wartime stories most recounted are those of narrow escapes and miraculous survivals, there are many more which were less palatable. Rescue parties tried to spare people the grief of seeing their dead relatives pulled from the rubble. Some bodies had been crushed or torn apart in the blast, or burned while trapped under fallen debris. In Winchester Grove, Mr Chatsworth was told not to look as his sister's body was freed, although he was reassured that she was 'all there'.

Ninety-four men, women and children were killed in York that night, in a raid which lasted around ninety minutes. A total of 579 houses were rendered uninhabitable, with a further 2,500 damaged. According to Charles Whiting in his book *The Great York Air Raid 1942*, it was 'the greatest blood-letting and destruction in York's recent history.' Sixty-nine high explosive bombs were dropped (ten of which did

Henry Milner memorial on Platform 3 at York Station.

not explode) and many more incendiary bombs. Six of the German aircrew were also killed that night, all young men in their early twenties.

The sight of those familiar York landmarks which had survived the night unscathed was probably one of the things which gave people the strength to carry on the next day. For one lady mentioned by Charles Whiting, it was, 'Bootham Bar, gleaming white and undamaged in the sunlight', and for many, it will have been the Minster, miraculously spared by the Germans.

According to a report in the *Yorkshire Observer*, people were going about their business the next day as usual, in true wartime spirit. 'They might have been a holiday crowd, walking out in the sunshine,' the reporter commented. 'I have seen people looking much less happy at Blackpool.' York continued on, just as it had done, no matter what the circumstances, for more than 2,000 years.

THE BAEDECKER RAIDS

The Baedecker Raids were a series of German air attacks on historic English towns. They were carried out in retaliation for the RAF's bombing of historic Lübeck on 28/29 March 1942, which caused a firestorm and led to the destruction of three of Lübeck's main churches. The targets for German revenge were reputedly selected from the Baedecker tourist guide to Great Britain (hence the name). Along with York, the towns of Exeter, Bath, Norwich and Canterbury were bombed during the raids. As well as historic buildings, there were also strategic targets in the raid on York: the station, the carriageworks, and Clifton airfield.

Visit our website and discover thousands of other History Press books.

www.thehistorypress.co.uk